The Standard for English Grammar Books

GRAMMAR ZONE
WORKBOOK

ZONE

입문편

GRAMMAR ZONE
WORKBOOK 입문편

지은이	NE능률 영어교육연구소
선임연구원	한정은
연구원	박진향 정희은 이은비 강혜진 김은경 신유승
영문교열	Benjamin Robinson Patrick Ferraro
표지 · 내지디자인	닷츠
내지일러스트	박응식
맥편집	이인선
영업	한기영 이경구 박인규 정철교 하진수 김남준 이우현
마케팅	박혜선 남경진 이지원 김여진
원고에 도움을 주신 분	구희진

Copyright ⓒ 2017 by NE Neungyule, Inc.

All rights reserved. No part of this publication may be reproduced, stored in a retrieval system, or transmitted in any form or by any means, electronic, mechanical, photocopying, recording, or otherwise, without the prior permission of the copyright owner.

✖ 본 교재의 독창적인 내용에 대한 일체의 무단 전재 · 모방은 법률로 금지되어 있습니다.

◆ 파본은 구매처에서 교환 가능합니다.

NE능률이
미래를
창조합니다.

건강한 배움의 고객가치를 제공하겠다는 꿈을 실현하기 위해
42년 동안 열심히 달려왔습니다.

앞으로도 끊임없는 연구와 노력을 통해
당연한 것을 멈추지 않고

고객, 기업, 직원 모두가 함께 성장하는 NE능률이 되겠습니다.

NE 능률

NE능률의 모든 교재가 한 곳에 - 엔이 북스

NE_Books

www.nebooks.co.kr ▼

NE능률의 유초등 교재부터 중고생 참고서,
토익·토플 수험서와 일반 영어까지!
PC는 물론 태블릿 PC, 스마트폰으로 언제 어디서나
NE능률의 교재와 다양한 학습 자료를 만나보세요.

✓ 필요한 부가 학습 자료 바로 찾기
✓ 주요 인기 교재들을 한눈에 확인
✓ 나에게 딱 맞는 교재를 찾아주는 스마트 검색
✓ 함께 보면 좋은 교재와 다음 단계 교재 추천
✓ 회원 가입, 교재 후기 작성 등 사이트 활동 시 NE Point 적립

건강한
배움의 즐거움

NE 능률

영어교과서 리딩튜터 능률보카 빠른독해 바른독해 수능만만 월등한 개념 수학 유형 더블
NE_Build & Grow   NE_Times   NE_Kids(굿잡,상상수프)   NE_능률 주니어랩   아이챌린지

Practice is the best of all instructions.

연습은 가장 좋은 가르침이다.

———

유명한 운동 선수, 최고의 과학자, 노벨상을 받은 작가, 그 누구도 자신들이 이루어낸 것이 하루 아침에 완성되었다고 말하는 사람은 없습니다. 그들을 성공으로 이끈 것은 무엇일까요? 여러분도 알다시피 목표를 달성하고 꿈을 이루는 데 성실하게 연습하는 것만큼 효과적인 무기는 없습니다. 저희는 여러분을 '문법 지존(至尊)'의 세계로 인도할 수 있는 가장 좋은 무기를 준비하였습니다. G-ZONE에서 학습한 모든 것을 이 WORKBOOK을 통해 연습하여 여러분 모두 문법의 '지존'이 되길 바랍니다. 꾸준한 연습을 다짐하는 여러분을 응원합니다.

구성과 특징

TEST

각 UNIT을 제대로 학습하였는지 확인할 수 있는 다양한 유형의 문제를 수록하였습니다. 비교적 간단한 드릴형 문제에서부터 사고력과 응용력을 요하는 문제까지 꼼꼼히 풀어본 후 부족한 부분에 대해 추가 학습 계획을 세워 봅시다.

CHECK UP

각 UNIT의 핵심 문법을 간단한 문제를 통해 확인할 수 있습니다. 각 문제 옆에는 해당 문법을 다룬 본 교재의 항목이 표시되어 있으므로, 추가 학습이 필요하다면 해당 항목을 복습한 후 Workbook으로 돌아오세요.

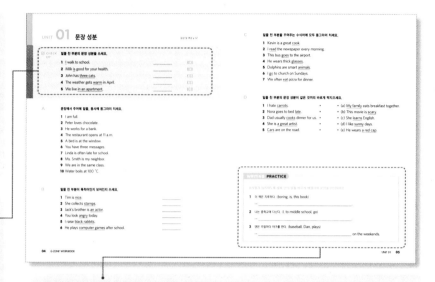

WRITING PRACTICE 쓰기 연습이 가능한 문제를 충분히 제시하였습니다. 수행평가나 서술형 문제 대비가 가능하며 궁극적으로 영어 쓰기 실력을 향상시켜 줍니다.

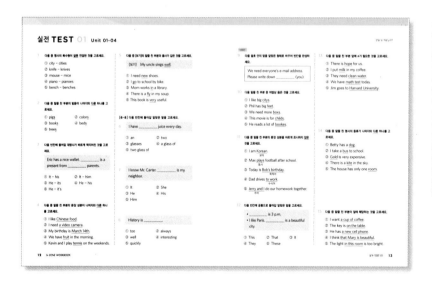

실전 TEST

여러 UNIT의 문법 사항을 종합적으로 확인할 수 있도록 총 6회의 실전 TEST를 제공합니다. 중간고사 및 기말고사에 대비할 수 있도록 문제 유형과 난이도 등을 실제에 맞추어 구성하였으며, 실제 기출을 응용한 주관식 문제를 제시하여 수행평가 및 서술형 문제 대비에도 유용합니다.

Contents

CHECK UP

밑줄 친 부분의 문장 성분을 쓰세요.

1 <u>I</u> walk to school. _____ `A`

2 Milk <u>is</u> good for your health. _____ `A`

3 John has <u>three cats</u>. _____ `B-1`

4 The weather gets <u>warm</u> in April. _____ `B-2`

5 We live <u>in an apartment</u>. _____ `C`

A 문장에서 주어에 밑줄, 동사에 동그라미 치세요.

1 I am full.

2 Peter loves chocolate.

3 He works for a bank.

4 The restaurant opens at 11 a.m.

5 A bird is at the window.

6 You have three messages.

7 Linda is often late for school.

8 Ms. Smith is my neighbor.

9 We are in the same class.

10 Water boils at 100 °C.

B 밑줄 친 부분이 목적어인지 보어인지 쓰세요.

1 Tim is <u>nice</u>. _____

2 She collects <u>stamps</u>. _____

3 Jack's brother is <u>an actor</u>. _____

4 You look <u>angry</u> today. _____

5 I raise <u>black rabbits</u>. _____

6 He plays <u>computer games</u> after school. _____

C 밑줄 친 부분을 꾸며주는 수식어에 모두 동그라미 치세요.

1 Kevin is a great cook.

2 I read the newspaper every morning.

3 This bus goes to the airport.

4 He wears thick glasses.

5 Dolphins are smart animals.

6 I go to church on Sundays.

7 We often eat pizza for dinner.

D 밑줄 친 부분의 문장 성분이 같은 것끼리 바르게 짝지으세요.

1 I hate carrots. •
2 Nora goes to bed late. •
3 Dad usually cooks dinner for us. •
4 She is a great artist. •
5 Cars are on the road. •

• (a) My family eats breakfast together.
• (b) This movie is scary.
• (c) She learns English.
• (d) I like sunny days.
• (e) He wears a red cap.

WRITING PRACTICE

우리말과 일치하도록 괄호 안의 말을 바르게 배열하여 문장을 완성하세요.

1 이 책은 지루하다. (boring, is, this book)

→ _____.

2 나는 중학교에 다닌다. (I, to middle school, go)

→ _____.

3 댄은 주말마다 야구를 한다. (baseball, Dan, plays)

→ _____ on the weekends.

☑ CHECK UP   **밑줄 친 부분의 품사를 쓰세요.**

1 This book is <u>interesting</u>.   _____   A

2 I <u>go</u> to the gym every day.   _____   A

3 We need more <u>time</u>.   _____   A

4 The room is nice <u>and</u> clean.   _____   A

5 My father <u>usually</u> goes to work early.   _____   A

A   **밑줄 친 부분의 품사에 해당하는 것을 [보기]에서 골라 쓰세요.**

[보기]   동사   명사   대명사   형용사   부사   전치사   접속사   감탄사

1 <u>That</u> is our house.   _____

2 I like your <u>new</u> shoes.   _____

3 <u>Jordan</u> is a police officer.   _____

4 Do you like coffee <u>or</u> tea?   _____

5 He is popular <u>at</u> school.   _____

6 Today <u>is</u> my birthday.   _____

7 <u>Oops</u>, I am sorry.   _____

8 I like <u>spicy</u> food.   _____

9 My <u>computer</u> is very old.   _____

10 I <u>have</u> a headache.   _____

11 Thank you <u>for</u> the gift.   _____

12 He is <u>very</u> tall.   _____

13 <u>Oh</u>, this is wonderful!   _____

14 She can speak English <u>well</u>.   _____

15 Amy is a nurse. <u>She</u> helps sick people.   _____

16 I always take the subway <u>because</u> it is fast.   _____

B   밑줄 친 부분이 구인지 절인지 쓰세요.

1 (1) Alex lives <u>in a city</u>. _____

    (2) Alex lives in a city, <u>and Joe lives in the country</u>. _____

2 (1) I know the man <u>in this picture</u>. _____

    (2) I know <u>that he is from Canada</u>. _____

3 (1) She eats dinner <u>when school is over</u>. _____

    (2) She eats dinner <u>after school</u>. _____

C   자연스러운 한 문장이 되도록 절과 절을 바르게 짝지으세요.

1 I think •   • (a) when I get home.

2 Tom likes juice •   • (b) and it is 10 years old.

3 I take a shower •   • (c) that your idea is great.

4 Jessica has a cat •   • (d) but he doesn't like coffee.

5 I eat vegetables •   • (e) because they are good for my health.

WRITING PRACTICE

우리말과 일치하도록 괄호 안의 말을 바르게 배열하여 문장을 완성하세요.

1 폴은 런던에 산다. (lives, in, Paul)

→ _____ London.

2 가족은 나에게 매우 중요하다. (important, is, very)

→ Family _____ to me.

3 나는 내일 시험이 있어서 긴장된다. (a test, I, because, have)

→ I am nervous _____ tomorrow.

UNIT 03 명사

↗ CHECK UP **괄호 안에서 알맞은 것을 고르세요.**

1 I need (pen / a pen). A-1

2 I have (a idea / an idea). A-1

3 He has three (childs / children). A-2

4 We want (happiness / a happiness) C-1

5 She drinks (two teas / two cups of tea) every night. C-2

A 그림과 일치하도록 [보기]의 명사를 알맞은 형태로 바꾸어 빈칸을 완성하세요.

[보기] foot   woman   tomato   leaf   dish   flower

1
a _____   two _____

2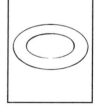
a _____   three _____

3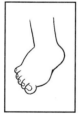
a _____   two _____

4
a _____   two _____

5
a _____   three _____

6
a _____   four _____

B 밑줄 친 부분 중 어법상 옳은 것에 ○ 표시하고, 옳지 않은 것은 바르게 고쳐 쓰세요.

1 I want some <u>waters</u>. _____

2 Wendy has good <u>friends</u>. _____

3 He has <u>a apple</u> every morning. _____

4 We have two <u>potatos</u>. _____

5 She lives in <u>a Seoul</u>. _____

6 I need three <u>boxes</u>. _____

7 <u>Health</u> is important. _____

C [보기]에서 알맞은 명사를 골라 적절한 형태로 바꾸어 빈칸을 완성하세요.

[보기]   glass   piece   cup   slice

1 I need five _____ of paper.

2 James has a _____ of orange juice with breakfast.

3 I put two _____ of ham on my sandwich.

4 Mom drinks three _____ of coffee every day.

WRITING PRACTICE

우리말과 일치하도록 괄호 안의 말을 바르게 배열하여 문장을 완성하세요.

1 나는 우산이 하나 필요하다. (an, need, I, umbrella)

→ _____.

2 내 어린 여동생은 이가 네 개다. (teeth, my, four, has, baby sister)

→ _____.

3 그는 매일 아침 물 한 잔을 마신다. (a, of, water, glass, drinks)

→ He _____ every morning.

☑ CHECK UP **괄호 안에서 알맞은 것을 고르세요.**

1 Ms. Jones is a teacher. (She / They) teaches math. [A]

2 I know (him / his) very well. [A]

3 This is not (my / mine). It is (your / yours) book. [A]

4 (That / Those) shoes are expensive. [B]

5 (It / This) is rainy today. [C]

A **[보기]에서 알맞은 대명사를 골라 적절한 형태로 바꾸어 빈칸을 완성하세요.**

[보기]   I   we   you   he   she   it   they

1 My brother is a cook. _____ cooks Italian food.

2 I have a diary. _____ cover is green.

3 Nick is in Sydney now. We miss _____.

4 We love Mr. Jackson. _____ class is fun.

5 Beijing is the capital of China. _____ is a huge city.

6 Chris and I know each other. _____ go to the same church.

7 I want a new cell phone. _____ is too old.

8 We have a problem. Please help _____.

9 Jane loves Korean food. Bulgogi is _____ favorite.

10 Dan has a nice watch. I want a watch like _____.

11 Amy lives next door. I see _____ every morning.

12 We have trees in our yard. _____ leaves are yellow now.

B 그림과 일치하도록 [보기]에서 알맞은 말을 하나씩 골라 빈칸을 채우세요.

[보기]   this   that   these   those

1

_____ are letters for you.

2

_____ is a zebra.

3

_____ is my brother, Paul.

4

_____ are nice bags.

WRITING PRACTICE

우리말과 일치하도록 [보기]와 괄호 안의 말을 이용하여 빈칸을 완성하세요.

[보기]   we   it   they   these

1 나는 개가 두 마리 있다. 그것들은 2살이다. (are)

→ I have two dogs. _____ _____ two years old.

2 이것들은 내가 가장 좋아하는 책들이다. (are)

→ _____ _____ my favorite books.

3 나는 수업에 늦었다. 벌써 8시이다. (is)

→ I am late for class. _____ _____ already 8 o'clock.

4 수잔과 나는 친한 친구이다. 우리는 방과 후에 매일 만난다. (meet)

→ Susan and I are close friends. _____ _____ every day after school.

실전 TEST 01 Unit 01-04

1 다음 중 명사의 복수형이 <u>잘못</u> 연결된 것을 고르세요.

① city – cities
② knife – knives
③ mouse – mice
④ piano – pianoes
⑤ bench – benches

2 다음 중 밑줄 친 부분의 발음이 나머지와 <u>다른</u> 하나를 고르세요.

① pig<u>s</u>
② color<u>s</u>
③ book<u>s</u>
④ bed<u>s</u>
⑤ tree<u>s</u>

3 다음 빈칸에 들어갈 대명사가 바르게 짝지어진 것을 고르세요.

Eric has a nice wallet. _____ is a present from _____ parents.

① It – his
② It – him
③ He – its
④ He – his
⑤ He – it's

4 다음 중 밑줄 친 부분의 문장 성분이 나머지와 <u>다른</u> 하나를 고르세요.

① I like <u>Chinese food</u>.
② I need <u>a video camera</u>.
③ My birthday is <u>March 14th</u>.
④ We have <u>fruit</u> in the morning.
⑤ Kevin and I play <u>tennis</u> on the weekends.

5 다음 중 [보기]의 밑줄 친 부분과 품사가 같은 것을 고르세요.

[보기] My uncle sings <u>well</u>.

① I need <u>new</u> shoes.
② I <u>go</u> to school by bike.
③ Mom works <u>in</u> a library.
④ There is a <u>fly</u> in my soup.
⑤ This book is <u>very</u> useful.

[6-8] 다음 빈칸에 들어갈 알맞은 말을 고르세요.

6 I have _____ juice every day.

① an
② two
③ glasses
④ a glass of
⑤ two glass of

7 I know Mr. Carter. _____ is my neighbor.

① It
② She
③ He
④ His
⑤ Him

8 History is _____.

① too
② always
③ well
④ interesting
⑤ quickly

9 다음 괄호 안의 말을 알맞은 형태로 바꾸어 빈칸을 완성하세요.

> We need everyone's e-mail address.
> Please write down _____ (you).

10 다음 밑줄 친 부분 중 어법상 옳은 것을 고르세요.

① I like big <u>citys</u>.
② Phil has big <u>feet</u>.
③ We need more <u>boxs</u>.
④ This movie is for <u>childs</u>.
⑤ He reads a lot of <u>bookes</u>.

11 다음 중 밑줄 친 부분의 문장 성분을 바르게 표시하지 <u>않은</u> 것을 고르세요.

① I am <u>Korean</u>.
        보어
② Max <u>plays</u> football after school.
      동사
③ Today is <u>Bob's birthday</u>.
         목적어
④ Dad drives <u>to work</u>.
        수식어
⑤ <u>Jerry and I</u> do our homework together.
  주어

12 다음 빈칸에 공통으로 들어갈 알맞은 말을 고르세요.

> • _____ is 3 p.m.
> • I like Paris. _____ is a beautiful city.

① This   ② That   ③ It
④ They   ⑤ These

13 다음 중 밑줄 친 부분 앞에 a가 필요한 것을 고르세요.

① There is <u>hope</u> for us.
② I put <u>milk</u> in my coffee.
③ They need <u>clean water</u>.
④ We have <u>math test</u> today.
⑤ Jim goes to <u>Harvard University</u>.

14 다음 중 밑줄 친 명사의 종류가 나머지와 <u>다른</u> 하나를 고르세요.

① Betty has a <u>dog</u>.
② I take a <u>bus</u> to school.
③ <u>Gold</u> is very expensive.
④ There is a <u>kite</u> in the sky.
⑤ The house has only one <u>room</u>.

15 다음 중 밑줄 친 부분이 절에 해당하는 것을 고르세요.

① I want <u>a cup of coffee</u>.
② The key is <u>on the table</u>.
③ He has <u>a new cell phone</u>.
④ I think <u>that Mary is beautiful</u>.
⑤ The light <u>in this room</u> is too bright.

16 ① We need <u>three chairs</u>.
   ② Take <u>a piece of paper</u>.
   ③ <u>Two glasses of milk</u>, please.
   ④ We have <u>five people</u> in our family.
   ⑤ I have <u>two breads</u> for breakfast.

17 ① <u>This</u> is my friend Luca.
   ② <u>This</u> street is dangerous.
   ③ I like <u>that</u> beautiful song.
   ④ <u>This</u> car looks perfect.
   ⑤ <u>That</u> books are funny.

18 ① Follow <u>us</u>.
   ② Open <u>your</u> book to page 17.
   ③ I love <u>he's</u> smile.
   ④ He has a cat. <u>It</u> has a long tail.
   ⑤ I have pens. You can use <u>them</u>.

19 다음 중 밑줄 친 부분의 품사가 나머지와 <u>다른</u> 하나를 고르세요.
   ① Mike is <u>very</u> smart.
   ② He wants a <u>new</u> TV.
   ③ I am often <u>late</u> for school.
   ④ The weather is <u>strange</u> these days.
   ⑤ Vegetables are <u>good</u> for your health.

20 다음 중 밑줄 친 부분의 성격이 나머지와 <u>다른</u> 하나를 고르세요.
   ① I am sad <u>when it rains</u>.
   ② Your bag is <u>on the sofa</u>.
   ③ We believe <u>that the Earth is round</u>.
   ④ I like chocolate cake <u>because it is delicious</u>.
   ⑤ Andy is my best friend, <u>and we have the same hobby</u>.

21 다음 중 수식어와 그것이 꾸며주는 말을 바르게 나타내지 <u>않은</u> 것을 고르세요.
   ① Terry is a <u>good cook</u>.
   ② This pizza is <u>too big</u>.
   ③ She has a <u>handsome boyfriend</u>.
   ④ Grapes are my <u>favorite fruit</u>.
   ⑤ He <u>gets up early</u> in the morning.

22 다음 중 [보기]의 밑줄 친 It과 쓰임이 <u>다른</u> 하나를 고르세요.

[보기] <u>It</u> is 10 o'clock.

   ① <u>It</u> is Friday.
   ② <u>It</u> is August 18th.
   ③ <u>It</u> is a great movie.
   ④ <u>It</u> is windy outside.
   ⑤ <u>It</u> is a kilometer to the station.

23   The hotel has _____.

① a pool   ② very cheap
③ ten floors   ④ many rooms
⑤ seven elevators

24   Tim works _____.

① slowly   ② office
③ fast   ④ hard
⑤ carefully

25   _____ dog is six years old.

① My   ② His
③ This   ④ These
⑤ That

26 다음 밑줄 친 부분이 꾸며주는 단어의 품사가 [보기]와 다른 하나를 고르세요.

   [보기] I <u>always</u> think about my future.

① Amy studies <u>hard</u>.
② Chris takes a lesson <u>at 7 o'clock</u>.
③ They go <u>to the same school</u>.
④ I <u>sometimes</u> drink green tea.
⑤ The books <u>in this box</u> are mine.

[27-29] 다음 우리말과 일치하도록 빈칸에 알맞은 말을 써서 대화를 완성하세요.

27 | A : 오늘이 무슨 요일이지?
     What day is it today?
   B : 수요일이야.
     _____ _____ _____.

28 | A : 이것이 네 시계니?
     Is this your watch?
   B : 아니. 그것은 우리 어머니 것이야.
     No. It's my _____ watch.

29 | A : 전 케이크 한 조각 주세요.
     I will have _____ _____
     _____ cake.
   B : 저도 같은 것으로 주세요.
     Same thing for me, please.

30 다음 밑줄 친 부분 중 어법상 바르게 고치지 <u>않은</u> 것을 고르세요.

① <u>An air</u> is important to us. (→ Air)
② He eats <u>an banana</u> every day.
   (→ a banana)
③ <u>A cups of teas</u> for me, please. (→ A cup of tea)
④ I write <u>a lot of e-mail</u> every day. (→ a lot of e-mails)
⑤ We need <u>ten papers</u>. (→ ten pieces of papers)

UNIT 05 be동사 I

☑ CHECK UP   괄호 안에서 알맞은 것을 고르세요.

1 We (am / are) ready for the show.   `A`

2 English (is / are) fun.   `A`

3 (They're / Their) my classmates.   `A`

4 There (is / are) a red car on the road.   `B`

5 There (is / are) roses in my garden.   `B`

A   문장의 빈칸에 알맞은 be동사의 현재형을 쓰세요.

1 Jill and Kate _____ twins.

2 My computer _____ slow.

3 Her hair _____ very short.

4 These pants _____ dirty.

5 She _____ from France.

6 I _____ in the sixth grade.

7 There _____ a big tree in my yard.

8 There _____ five people in the room.

9 You _____ nice to me.

10 Its ears _____ big.

B   이어질 말로 알맞은 것을 짝지으세요.

1 His name   •   • (a) are late for class again.

2 The stories   •   • (b) is Henry Oh.

3 David and you   •   • (c) is a great artist.

4 Ms. Choi   •   • (d) are long.

C [보기]에서 알맞은 말을 골라 빈칸을 채우세요.

[보기]   the story   five benches   an apple   they

1 _____ are my parents.
2 There is _____ on the kitchen table.
3 _____ is about a rabbit and a turtle.
4 There are _____ in the park.

D 빈칸에 is 또는 are를 넣어 글을 완성하세요.

1 There (1) _____ a river near my house. Every summer my brother and I swim in the river. It (2) _____ a lot of fun. My parents (3) _____ good swimmers, too. We have fun together.

2 There (1) _____ many trees by the river. They (2) _____ old and tall. My brother (3) _____ a brave boy. He sometimes climbs up the trees.

WRITING PRACTICE

우리말과 일치하도록 괄호 안의 말을 이용하여 문장을 완성하세요.

1 수학은 내가 가장 좋아하는 과목이다. (math)

→ _____ _____ my favorite subject.

2 이 시험에는 25개의 문제가 있다. (there)

→ _____ _____ 25 questions on this test.

3 냉장고에 우유가 있다. (there)

→ _____ _____ milk in the fridge.

4 그것의 가격은 지금 3달러이다. (it, price)

→ _____ _____ _____ three dollars now.

☑ **CHECK UP**   **괄호 안에서 알맞은 것을 고르세요.**

1 (You're / Your) not alone.   `A`

2 The hotel (isn't / aren't) near the station.   `A`

3 (I am / Am I) a good singer?   `B`

4 There (isn't / aren't) any problems.   `C`

5 (There are / Are there) old letters in the box?   `C`

A   **질문에 대한 대답이 자연스럽게 이어지도록 괄호 안에서 알맞은 것을 고르세요.**

1 A: Is this bag yours?

B: Yes, (it is / it isn't).

2 A: Are you good at basketball?

B: No, (I am / I'm not).

3 A: Is there a cup of coffee?

B: Yes, (there is / there isn't).

4 A: Are there any questions for him?

B: No, (there are / there aren't).

5 A: Is the actor very talented?

B: Yes, (he is / he isn't).

6 A: Am I the first visitor today?

B: Yes, (you are / you aren't).

B   **괄호 안의 말을 바르게 배열하여 대화를 완성하세요.**

1 A: _____ _____ (you, are) Jenny?

B: No, I'm not. I am Sarah.

2 A: _____ _____ (Peter, is) from Canada?

B: Yes, he is.

3 A: _____ _____ _____ (these, are, questions) difficult?

B: No, they aren't. They are very easy.

C 그림과 일치하도록 「There is[are] ~」를 써서 대화를 완성하세요.

1

A: _____ _____ a picture on the wall?

B: _____, _____ _____.

2

A: _____ _____ many books on the desk?

B: _____, _____ _____.

3

A: _____ _____ a dog under the table?

B: _____, _____ _____.

There is a cat under the table.

4

A: _____ _____ 31 days in November?

B: _____, _____ _____.

There are 30 days in November.

WRITING PRACTICE

우리말과 일치하도록 괄호 안의 말을 바르게 배열하여 문장을 완성하세요.

1 나는 고등학생이 아니다. (not, student, am, a, I, high school)

→ _____.

2 책상 위에 노트가 한 권 있나요? (a notebook, is, on the desk, there)

→ _____?

3 저 아이들은 네 친구들이니? (friends, children, are, those, your)

→ _____?

↗ CHECK UP | 괄호 안에서 알맞은 것을 고르세요.

1 I (like / likes) chocolate.   A
2 Kevin (play / plays) the guitar.   A
3 My sister (go / goes) to elementary school.   A
4 He (catchs / catches) a cold very often.   B
5 She (haves / has) a great camera.   B

A   괄호 안의 동사를 현재형으로 바꾸어 빈칸을 완성하세요.

1 He _____ (drive) to work.
2 They _____ (leave) home very early.
3 The sun _____ (rise) in the east.
4 I _____ (get) up at 7:30 in the morning.
5 Jinho _____ (love) comic books.
6 He and his brother _____ (like) hip-hop music.
7 We _____ (take) a walk after dinner.
8 His sister _____ (have) a beautiful smile.
9 Tom _____ (study) every night.
10 My mom _____ (teach) the piano.

B   [보기]에서 알맞은 동사를 골라 현재형으로 바꾸어 문장을 완성하세요.

[보기]   walk   read   learn   have

1 I _____ to school.
2 Ms. Rogers _____ English.
3 We _____ a small garden.
4 Alex _____ the newspaper in the morning.

C 　　주어진 동사를 현재형으로 바꾸어 빈칸을 완성하세요.

1 speak

(1) We _____ Korean.

(2) Jihong _____ three languages.

2 have

(1) They _____ three pets.

(2) He _____ five cups of coffee every day.

3 go

(1) This train _____ to Busan.

(2) I _____ to school by bus.

4 cry

(1) Babies _____.

(2) Nora _____ very often.

5 wash

(1) This washing machine _____ clothes well.

(2) I _____ my car every Sunday.

WRITING PRACTICE

우리말과 일치하도록 괄호 안의 말을 이용하여 문장을 완성하세요.

1 우리 학교는 오전 8시에 시작한다. (my school, start)

→ _____

2 나는 새 가방이 필요하다. (I, need)

→ _____

3 그는 온라인으로 책을 산다. (buy, books)

→ _____

↗ CHECK
  UP
괄호 안에서 알맞은 것을 고르세요.

1 I (am not / don't) eat breakfast.　　　　　　　　　　　　　A

2 Jake (don't / doesn't) like big cities.　　　　　　　　　　　A

3 (Are / Do) we have enough time?　　　　　　　　　　　　B

4 (Do / Does) he usually come home late?　　　　　　　　　B

5 A: Does Linda go to church?　　　　　　　　　　　　　　B

　　B : No, she (don't / doesn't).

A　**괄호 안의 말을 이용하여 부정문을 완성하세요.**

1 I share a room with my sister.

　I _____ _____ (not, have) my own room.

2 You look like your father.

　You _____ _____ (not, look) like your mother.

3 Mark reads news online.

　He _____ _____ (not, read) newspapers.

4 Marie lives with her parents.

　She _____ _____ (not, live) alone.

B　**괄호 안의 말을 이용하여 대화를 완성하세요.**

1 A: _____ _____ _____ (you, walk) to school?

　B : No, I don't. I go to school by bike.

2 A: _____ _____ _____ _____ (the shop, open) on Sundays?

　B : Yes, it does.

3 A: _____ _____ _____ (he, work) at a restaurant?

　B : No, he doesn't. He works at the post office.

C 주어진 동사를 써서 각각 부정문과 의문문을 완성하세요. (현재형으로 쓸 것)

1 need

(1) You _____ _____ an umbrella today.

(2) _____ I _____ a passport?

2 have

(1) Andrew _____ _____ a cell phone.

(2) _____ you _____ time now?

3 like

(1) They _____ _____ action movies.

(2) _____ Dave _____ spicy food?

4 know

(1) He _____ _____ my name.

(2) _____ she _____ my e-mail address?

5 use

(1) Wendy _____ _____ shampoo.

(2) _____ they _____ the Internet?

WRITING PRACTICE

우리말과 일치하도록 [보기]와 괄호 안의 동사를 이용하여 문장을 완성하세요.

[보기]   do   don't   doesn't

1 우리 아버지는 담배를 피우지 않으신다. (smoke)

→ My father _____ _____.

2 이슬람교도들은 돼지고기를 먹지 않는다. (eat)

→ Muslims _____ _____ pork.

3 A: 너는 토요일마다 수업이 있니?   B: 아니, 없어. (have)

→ A: _____ _____ _____ classes on Saturdays?   B: No, I don't.

정답 및 해설 p.14

☑ CHECK UP **괄호 안에서 알맞은 것을 고르세요.**

1 When (is / are) your birthday? `A·1`

2 What (do / does) Jason do? `A·2`

3 (Where / When) are you from? `B·1`

4 A: (What / Why) is this room so hot? `B·3`
   B: Because the air conditioner is broken.

5 (Who / Whose) cell phone is this? `B·5`

A **괄호 안의 말을 이용하여 대화를 완성하세요.**

1 A: _____ _____ my glasses? (where, be)
   B: They are in the bathroom.

2 A: _____ _____ you _____ after school? (what, do)
   B: I usually play baseball.

3 A: _____ _____ the train _____? (when, arrive)
   B: It arrives at 9:45.

4 A: _____ _____ they _____ you? (how, know)
   B: We are classmates.

5 A: _____ _____ your favorite season? (which, be)
   B: I like winter.

6 A: _____ _____ Harry _____? (where, live)
   B: He lives in London.

7 A: _____ _____ _____ it today? (what day, be)
   B: It's Monday.

8 A: _____ _____ _____ _____ this building _____?
   (how many floors, have)
   B: It has five floors.

B 그림과 일치하도록 빈칸에 알맞은 말을 넣어 대화를 완성하세요.

1

A: _____ _____ the key?

B: It is on the sofa.

2

A: _____ _____ the answer?

B: I know the answer.

3

A: _____ _____ the concert _____?

B: It starts at 7:30 p.m.

4

A: _____ _____ you usually _____ for lunch?

B: I usually have a sandwich.

WRITING PRACTICE

우리말과 일치하도록 [보기]와 괄호 안의 동사를 이용하여 문장을 완성하세요.

[보기]   When   Who   Why

1 A: 저 남자는 누구니?   B: 그는 내 사촌 에드야. (be)

→ A: _____ _____ that guy?   B: He is my cousin Ed.

2 A: 그녀는 왜 항상 늦니?   B: 그녀는 아주 멀리 살기 때문이지. (be)

→ A: _____ _____ she always late?   B: Because she lives far away.

3 A: 그 버스는 언제 오니?   B: 버스는 오후 2시에 와. (come)

→ A: _____ _____ the bus _____?   B: It comes at 2 p.m.

☑ CHECK UP **괄호 안에서 알맞은 것을 고르세요.**

1 Andy (sleeps / likes). A

2 He goes (school / to school). A

3 I watch (TV / hard) in the evening. B

4 She (has / lends) me money. C

5 Mom gives (a gift me / me a gift) on my birthday. C

A   **문장이 어떤 구조로 이루어져 있는지 [보기]에서 골라 번호를 쓰세요.**

[보기]   ① 주어 + 동사   ② 주어 + 동사 + 목적어
         ③ 주어 + 동사 + 간접목적어 + 직접목적어

1 He hates me. _____

2 I drive very slowly. _____

3 She wants fresh food. _____

4 They work here. _____

5 Laura smiles beautifully. _____

6 We play football after school. _____

7 Mr. Kim teaches us Japanese. _____

8 He goes to the gym every day. _____

9 She likes old movies. _____

10 I have toast and butter for breakfast. _____

11 My baby brother cries a lot. _____

12 We live in the same city. _____

13 Cindy sings well. _____

14 He takes photographs. _____

15 She makes us delicious cookies. _____

16 Kevin sends me a card on Christmas every year. _____

B   [보기]에서 알맞은 동사를 골라 현재형으로 바꾸어 문장을 완성하세요.

        [보기]   clean   walk   buy

1 I _____ to school every day.

2 Eric _____ me flowers.

3 We _____ our house on the weekends.

        [보기]   work   order   lend

4 Jay _____ hard.

5 He often _____ me his comic books.

6 We sometimes _____ pizza for lunch.

C   자연스러운 한 문장이 되도록 바르게 짝지으세요.

1 We do   •   • (a) our homework together.

2 You run   •   • (b) me science.

3 Dave teaches   •   • (c) fast.

WRITING PRACTICE

우리말과 일치하도록 괄호 안의 말을 이용하여 문장을 완성하세요.

1 나는 늘 집에서 공부한다. (home, study, at)

    → I always _____ _____ _____.

2 내 여동생은 가끔 소설을 읽는다. (novels, read)

    → My little sister sometimes _____ _____.

3 그는 자주 나에게 점심을 사준다. (lunch, buy, me)

    → He often _____ _____ _____.

☑ CHECK UP **괄호 안에서 알맞은 것을 고르세요.**

1 He is (nice / nicely).　　　　　　　　　　　　　　 A

2 I feel (great / greatly).　　　　　　　　　　　　　 A

3 How does water (come / become) ice?　　　 A

4 She (wants / makes) me happy.　　　　　　　 B-1

5 My mom tells me (eat / to eat) healthy food.　 B-2

A　**문장이 어떤 구조로 이루어져 있는지 [보기]에서 골라 번호를 쓰세요.**

[보기]　① 주어 + 동사 + 보어　　　　② 주어 + 동사 + 목적어 + 보어

1 I am Korean.　　　　　　　　　　　　　　　　　 _____

2 I feel sick now.　　　　　　　　　　　　　　　　 _____

3 My brother sometimes makes me crazy.　　　 _____

4 She turns red easily.　　　　　　　　　　　　　 _____

5 John is a police officer.　　　　　　　　　　　 _____

6 It gets dark early in winter.　　　　　　　　　 _____

7 I want him to clean his room.　　　　　　　　 _____

8 You look good with that new hair style.　　　 _____

9 Jim always asks me to help him with his homework.　 _____

B　**예시와 같이 밑줄 친 보어가 보충 설명하는 말에 동그라미 치세요.**

0 (This cake) tastes good.

1 You look great today.

2 She keeps her house clean.

3 Leaves turn red and yellow in fall.

4 He asked me to join his band.

C   [보기]에서 알맞은 동사를 골라 현재형으로 바꾸어 문장을 완성하세요.

> [보기]   call   be   want

1 She _____ the CEO of the company.

2 What do you _____ your dog?

3 I _____ you to call me tomorrow morning.

> [보기]   ask   make   smell

4 This soup _____ good.

5 Mom _____ me to clean my desk.

6 Science _____ our life comfortable.

D   괄호 안의 말을 이용하여 문장을 완성하세요.

1 That _____ _____! (amazing, sound)

2 These boots _____ _____ _____ _____.
(keep, warm, your feet)

3 My father always _____ _____ _____ _____ _____.
(save, tell, money, me, to)

WRITING PRACTICE

우리말과 일치하도록 괄호 안의 말을 바르게 배열하여 문장을 완성하세요.

1 아기들은 매일 튼튼해진다. (every day, grow, strong, babies)

→ _____.

2 우리는 그를 "빅"이라고 부른다. (call, we, "Big", him)

→ _____.

3 부모님은 내가 일찍 집에 오기를 원하신다. (to, home, me, want, come, early)

→ My parents _____.

실전 TEST 02 Unit 05-11

1 다음 빈칸에 들어갈 be동사가 바르게 짝지어진 것을 고르세요.

> • There _____ milk in the fridge.
> • There _____ 40 students in my class.

① are – is ② are – are
③ am – is ④ is – are
⑤ is – is

서술형

[2-3] 다음 주어진 동사를 알맞은 형태로 바꾸어 빈칸을 완성하세요.

2 watch

> I usually (1) _____ horror movies at a theater.
> Roy (2) _____ baseball games at home.

3 eat

> A: Joan (1) _____ too much fast food.
> B: How often does she (2) _____ it?
> A: Almost every day.

[4-7] 다음 밑줄 친 부분 중 어법상 옳지 않은 것을 고르세요.

4 ① I <u>am</u> hungry.
② This cookie <u>is</u> tasty.
③ You <u>are</u> very kind.
④ These pants <u>is</u> too short.
⑤ My grandmother <u>is</u> 70 years old.

5 ① You <u>aren't</u> a kid.
② I <u>amn't</u> wrong.
③ This <u>isn't</u> mine. It's hers.
④ They <u>aren't</u> twins.
⑤ It <u>isn't</u> Thursday. It's Friday.

6 ① Mom <u>loves</u> dogs.
② He <u>has</u> dinner at 7 p.m.
③ John <u>studys</u> Korean every day.
④ This store <u>sells</u> everything.
⑤ Mr. Lee <u>teaches</u> the violin.

7 ① There <u>are</u> three rooms on this floor.
② There <u>is</u> people in the living room.
③ There <u>is</u> a glass of water on the table.
④ There <u>is</u> a supermarket near my house.
⑤ There <u>are</u> beautiful flowers in the garden.

8 다음 두 문장이 같은 뜻이 되도록 빈칸에 알맞은 말을 고르세요.

> A cell phone is on the bed.
> = _____ a cell phone on the bed.

① Its
② Theirs
③ They are
④ There is
⑤ There are

9 다음 중 자연스럽지 <u>않은</u> 대화를 고르세요.

① A : How old are you?
　B : I'm 16 years old.
② A : Who do you look like?
　B : I look like my father.
③ A : Whose bag is this?
　B : It's me.
④ A : What day is it today?
　B : It's Tuesday.
⑤ A : When does the class start?
　B : It starts at 9 o'clock.

서술형

10 다음 빈칸에 알맞은 의문사를 쓰세요.

> A : _____ do you study English?
> B : Because it is fun.

[11-14] 다음 빈칸에 들어갈 알맞은 말을 고르세요.

11　A: Is Kevin from America?
　　B : _____ He is Australian.

① Yes, he is.
② Yes, it is.
③ No, he isn't.
④ No, it isn't.
⑤ No, they aren't.

12　A: Do you know his phone number?
　　B : _____

① Yes, I am.
② No, I am not.
③ Yes, I do.
④ No, you don't.
⑤ Yes, you do.

13　A: Does Paul work with you?
　　B : No, _____

① you do.
② he does.
③ you don't.
④ he don't.
⑤ he doesn't.

14　A: When does Amy leave home?
　　B : _____

① Yes, she does.
② She lives downtown.
③ Because her school is far away.
④ She leaves home at 8 a.m.
⑤ She takes the bus to school.

15 다음 중 문장의 구조가 [보기]와 <u>다른</u> 것을 고르세요.

[보기]   I like animals. (주어 + 동사 + 목적어)

① That sounds terrible.
② I need a thick coat.
③ Jack has five classes today.
④ She plays the piano after school.
⑤ We sometimes eat Chinese food for dinner.

16 다음 중 밑줄 친 동사의 종류가 [보기]와 같은 것을 고르세요.

[보기]   We go to the movies on the weekends.

① I work with Kelly.
② He sends me flowers on my birthday.
③ She has five cats.
④ Judy writes songs.
⑤ She makes people comfortable.

17 다음 빈칸에 들어갈 말이 바르게 짝지어진 것을 고르세요.

• We _____ a TV at home.
• Andrew _____ time now.

① aren't have – isn't have
② not have – not has
③ don't have – doesn't have
④ don't have – don't have
⑤ doesn't have – don't have

18 ① They <u>don't eat</u> meat.
② Mr. Smith <u>doesn't work</u> here.
③ She <u>doesn't have</u> a car.
④ I <u>don't know</u> his e-mail address.
⑤ The restaurant <u>don't open</u> on Mondays.

19 ① Mary <u>drives</u> to work.
② He <u>tells</u> me to study hard.
③ Jay's house <u>is</u> next to mine.
④ She <u>watches</u> good.
⑤ I <u>feed</u> my dog every day.

20 다음 중 질문에 대한 밑줄 친 대답이 <u>어색한</u> 것을 고르세요.

① A: Do you drive?
   B: <u>No, I don't.</u>
② A: Do you travel a lot?
   B: <u>Yes, I do.</u>
③ A: Does she work for a bank?
   B: <u>Yes, she does.</u>
④ A: Does Eric live in Tokyo?
   B: <u>No, he doesn't.</u>
⑤ A: Do Chinese people drink tea?
   B: <u>Yes, it does.</u>

21 다음 중 어법상 옳지 <u>않은</u> 것을 고르세요.

① Do you like winter?
② Does she keep a diary?
③ What does dogs eat?
④ When do you get up?
⑤ Where does he buy his clothes?

[22-25] 다음 빈칸에 들어갈 가장 알맞은 말을 고르세요.

22   The hotel _____ perfect for us.

① gives   ② walks   ③ sounds
④ tells   ⑤ wants

23   James _____ at the department store.

① works   ② makes   ③ feels
④ keeps   ⑤ calls

24   Ms. Brown _____ us science.

① studies   ② works   ③ has
④ teaches   ⑤ wants

25   My parents _____ me Princess.

① become   ② ask   ③ call
④ look   ⑤ teach

26 다음 중 목적어가 두 개인 문장을 고르세요.

① Sam always gives me advice.
② Mom wants me to get up early.
③ My son makes me happy.
④ I keep my nails clean.
⑤ They asked me to help them with their projects.

서술형

[27-28] 다음 우리말과 일치하도록 괄호 안의 말을 알맞은 형태로 바꾸어 문장을 완성하세요.

27   제니는 수학을 싫어한다. (not, like)

→ Jenny _____ _____ math.

28   밥을 어떻게 짓니? (cook)

→ _____ _____ you _____ rice?

서술형

[29-30] 다음 우리말과 일치하도록 빈칸에 알맞은 말을 쓰세요.

29   너는 오늘 행복해 보인다.

→ _____ _____ _____ today.

30   그녀는 그녀의 등을 곧게 유지한다.

→ She keeps _____ _____ _____.

CHECK UP 괄호 안에서 알맞은 것을 고르세요.

1 The Earth (goes / going) around the Sun. A

2 David (is / are) watching a baseball game. B-1

3 They (dance / are dancing) now. B-1

4 I (not am / am not) talking to you. C-1

5 A: Where (you are / are you) going? C-2

   B: I'm going to the supermarket.

A 괄호 안의 동사를 현재형으로 바꾸어 빈칸을 완성하세요.

1 You _____ (be) beautiful.

2 I _____ (read) books in bed at night.

3 A week _____ (have) seven days.

4 We _____ (live) in an apartment.

5 He _____ (take) piano lessons on Mondays.

6 The bus _____ (go) to Main Street.

7 They _____ (have) lunch at noon.

8 The bank _____ (close) at 4:30 p.m.

B 괄호 안의 말을 현재진행형으로 바꾸어 빈칸을 완성하세요.

1 He _____ _____ (read) a comic book.

   He _____ _____ _____ (not, study).

2 I _____ _____ (tell) the truth.

   I _____ _____ _____ (not, lie) to you.

3 The dogs _____ _____ (play) together.

   They _____ _____ _____ (not, fight).

그림과 일치하도록 [보기]의 동사를 현재진행형으로 바꾸어 대화를 완성하세요.

[보기] talk   do   go   read

1

A: _____ he _____ a
newspaper?
B : Yes, he is.

2

A: What _____ they _____ ?
B : They are taking pictures.

3

A: _____ Emily _____ on the
phone?
B : No, she isn't. She is writing an e-mail.

4

A: Where _____ they _____ ?
B : They are going to a coffee shop.

WRITING PRACTICE

우리말과 일치하도록 괄호 안의 말을 이용하여 문장을 완성하세요.

1 존은 지금 시험을 위해 공부하고 있다. (study)

→ John _____ _____ for a test now.

2 나뭇잎이 떨어지고 있다. (the leaves, fall)

→ _____ _____ _____ _____ .

3 그녀는 매일 아침에 머리를 빗는다. (comb, her hair)

→ She _____ _____ _____ every morning.

☑ CHECK
   UP
괄호 안에서 알맞은 것을 고르세요.

1 It (was / were) a sunny day. `A-1`

2 Tom (buys / bought) a new computer last weekend. `A-2`

3 She (looks / looked) tired this morning. `A-2`

4 They didn't (come / came) to school yesterday. `C-1`

5 A: Where (you went / did you go) last night? `C-2`

   B: We went to an Italian restaurant.

A   **주어진 동사를 현재시제 또는 과거시제로 바꾸어 빈칸을 완성하세요. (두 빈칸에 같은 시제를 쓰지 말 것)**

1 live
   (1) Lions _____ in Africa.
   (2) We _____ in Seoul two years ago.

2 be
   (1) She _____ in Canada now.
   (2) They _____ at a concert last night.

3 eat
   (1) Alex _____ cereal this morning.
   (2) Koreans _____ kimchi.

4 boil
   (1) She _____ an egg for lunch.
   (2) Water _____ at 100 ˚C.

5 study
   (1) I _____ Japanese these days.
   (2) Jim _____ for an English test yesterday.

B   괄호 안의 말을 과거형으로 바꾸어 빈칸을 완성하세요.

1 She _____ (make) a sweet chocolate cake.

2 I _____ (read) your e-mail this morning.

3 My grandfather _____ (die) two years ago.

4 Julie _____ _____ (not, come) to the party.

5 He _____ (not, be) in class yesterday.

6 We _____ _____ (not, know) about the news.

C   [보기]에서 알맞은 동사를 골라 과거시제의 대화를 완성하세요.

     [보기]   hear   be   do

1 A : _____ the movie good?

     B : No, it wasn't. It was boring.

2 A : _____ you _____ about the accident?

     B : Yes, I did.

3 A : What _____ you _____ on the weekend?

     B : I watched a movie.

WRITING PRACTICE

우리말과 일치하도록 괄호 안의 말을 알맞은 형태로 바꾸어 문장을 완성하세요.

1 나는 식당에서 내 영어 선생님을 봤다. (see)

→ _____ _____ _____ _____ _____ in a restaurant.

2 그는 나에게 친절했다. (be, kind)

→ _____ _____ _____ to me.

3 너는 어젯밤 언제 집에 왔니? (when, come)

→ _____ _____ _____ _____ _____ last night?

☑ CHECK UP **괄호 안에서 알맞은 것을 고르세요.**

1 It (is / will be) cold tomorrow. A-1

2 I (not will / will not) watch TV. A-2

3 Will Laura (come / comes) to the party? A-3

4 I am going (visit / to visit) Europe next month. B-1

5 A: What (you are going / are you going) to do today? B-3

    B : I'm going to read books.

A **[보기]의 말과 will을 이용하여 빈칸을 완성하세요.**

[보기]   win   call   not/take   rain   not/be   open

1 I _____ you later.

2 We _____ late again.

3 It _____ this afternoon.

4 Our team _____ the game.

5 The shop _____ at 10 a.m.

6 I _____ the subway to work today.

B **괄호 안의 말과 be going to를 이용하여 빈칸을 완성하세요.**

1 We _____ in the hotel. (stay)

2 I _____ him today. (not, see)

3 Tom _____ art in university. (study)

4 They _____ us tonight. (not, join)

5 Carl _____ Korea in April. (visit)

6 She _____ to Busan next week. (move)

7 We _____ Joe's birthday party tonight. (not, have)

C   **[보기]의 말과 괄호 안의 말을 이용하여 대화를 완성하세요.**

[보기]   be   when/leave   have   what/do

1 A: _____ you _____ dessert? (will)

B : No, thank you. I'm full.

2 A: _____ _____ you _____ this vacation? (will)

B : I'll go camping with my best friends.

3 A: _____ you _____ _____ _____ at home? (be going to)

B : Yes, I am. I'm tired.

4 A: _____ _____ we _____ _____ _____? (be going to)

B : We are going to leave tomorrow.

WRITING PRACTICE

우리말과 일치하도록 괄호 안의 말을 바르게 배열하여 문장을 완성하세요.

1 아델은 중국어를 배우려고 한다. (going, Chinese, is, learn, to)

→ Adele _____.

2 나는 컴퓨터 게임을 하지 않을 것이다. (play, not, computer games, will)

→ I _____.

3 이번 주말에 너는 무엇을 할 예정이니? (are, do, going to, what, you, this weekend)

→ _____?

☑ CHECK
UP

괄호 안에서 알맞은 것을 고르세요.

1 He (lived / has lived) in Korea since 2000.　A-1

2 I've known her (five years ago / for five years).　A-1

3 She (has lost / have lost) her wallet.　A-2

4 Ken (has just come / has just came) home.　A-2

5 A: Have you been to China?　C-2

　　B : No, I (didn't / haven't).

A　　**괄호 안의 동사를 현재완료형으로 바꾸어 빈칸을 완성하세요.**

1 Jenny _____ _____ (buy) a car.

2 I _____ _____ (be) to Europe twice.

3 He _____ _____ (forget) his homework.

4 I _____ _____ (not, read) this book before.

5 They _____ _____ (go) to Paris.

6 Ross _____ _____ (live) in London for three years.

7 I _____ just _____ (send) an e-mail to you.

8 My father _____ _____ (work) for the company for 15 years.

9 I _____ _____ (not, see) him since last year.

10 Lauren _____ never _____ (eat) kimchi.

B　　**두 문장이 같은 뜻이 되도록 빈칸을 완성하세요.**

1 They moved to Poland in 2015. They still live there.

　　= They _____ _____ in Poland since 2015.

2 I lost my cell phone yesterday. I still don't have it.

　　= I _____ _____ my cell phone.

3 He went to Barcelona. He is still in Barcelona.

　　= He _____ _____ to Barcelona.

C [보기]에서 알맞은 말을 골라 현재완료형으로 바꾸어 빈칸을 완성하세요.

[보기]   see   eat   not/do   go

1 Cindy _____ already _____ to bed.
2 We _____ just _____ dinner.
3 I _____ _____ my homework yet.
4 They _____ never _____ the man before.

D 괄호 안의 말을 알맞은 형태로 바꾸어 대화를 완성하세요.

1 A: _____ _____ _____ (you, be) to Japan?
   B: No, I haven't.
2 A: _____ _____ _____ (Eric, leave) home?
   B: Yes, he has.
3 A: _____ _____ _____ (you, finish) the report?
   B: Yes, I have.
4 A: How long _____ _____ _____ (she, study) in Austria?
   B: She has studied in Austria for three years.

WRITING PRACTICE

우리말과 일치하도록 괄호 안의 말을 알맞은 형태로 바꾸어 문장을 완성하세요.

1 우리 엄마께서는 같은 코트를 10년째 입으신다. (wear)

→ My mom _____ _____ the same coat for 10 years.

2 미아는 크로아티아에 가본 적이 한 번도 없다. (never, be)

→ Mia _____ _____ _____ to Croatia.

3 A: 너 이 영화 본 적 있니?   B: 아니, 없어. (watch)

→ A: _____ _____ _____ this movie?
   B: No, _____ _____.

UNIT 16 조동사 I

정답 및 해설 p.25

CHECK UP 괄호 안에서 알맞은 것을 고르세요.

1 Paul (can swim / can swims). `A-2`

2 They will (can / be able to) come to the party. `A-2`

3 It (will not rain / will doesn't rain) tomorrow. `A-3`

4 She (can't / couldn't) speak German last year. `B-1`

5 Can (I / me) have a cheeseburger, please? `B-2`

A 괄호 안의 말을 바르게 배열하여 문장을 완성하세요.

1 I _____. (run, fast, can)

2 Mike _____. (ski, can)

3 I _____. (cannot, French, speak)

4 Sally _____. (home, be, will, tonight, not)

5 _____? (can, the piano, you, play)

6 How _____? (I, weight, lose, can)

B 두 문장이 같은 뜻이 되도록 빈칸에 알맞은 말을 쓰세요.

1 I am not able to join you.

= I _____ _____ you.

2 Mary is able to play tennis.

= Mary _____ _____ tennis.

3 I was able to read without glasses.

= I _____ _____ without glasses.

4 Thomas wasn't able to go to school today.

= Thomas _____ _____ to school today.

C   그림과 일치하도록 괄호 안의 말을 이용하여 대화를 완성하세요.

1

A: _____ _____ _____
    me some money? (can, lend)

B: I'm sorry, but I can't.

2

A: _____ _____ _____
    your phone? (can, use)

B: No problem.

3

A: _____ _____ _____
    the door? (could, open)

B: Sure.

4

A: _____ _____ _____
    more rice? (could, have)

B: Of course.

WRITING PRACTICE

우리말과 일치하도록 [보기]와 괄호 안의 동사를 이용하여 문장을 완성하세요.

[보기]   could   couldn't   be able to

1 테리는 운전할 수 있다. (drive)

→ Terry _____.

2 나는 어젯밤 잠을 잘 수 없었다. (sleep)

→ I _____ last night.

3 A: 저를 역까지 태워주시겠어요?   B: 물론이죠. (take)

→ A: _____ to the station?   B: Sure.

UNIT 17 조동사 II

↗ CHECK UP **괄호 안에서 알맞은 것을 고르세요.**

1 A: (May / Must) I turn on the TV?   B: No problem.   `A-2`

2 Amy (must / had to) get up early the day before yesterday.   `B-1`

3 A: Must I buy a ticket? B: No, you (must not / don't have to).   `B-1`

4 He has worked too much. He (can't / must) be tired.   `B-2`

5 She (should / cannot) wear a thick coat because it's cold outside.   `C`

A **주어진 두 개의 조동사 중 하나를 골라, 괄호 안의 동사와 함께 빈칸을 완성하세요.**

1 may / may not
(1) Harry didn't come to school today. He _____ (be) sick.
(2) I have just seen her on the street. She _____ (be) at home.

2 may / must
(1) You _____ (keep) quiet in the library.
(2) The class is over. You _____ (go) now.

3 must / can't
(1) Ms. Smith _____ (be) 50 years old. She looks young.
(2) Jack has a expensive car. He _____ (be) rich.

4 must not / don't have to
(1) You _____ (run) in the hallway.
(2) It's Sunday. I _____ (go) to school today.

5 must / have to
(1) He lives far from his family. He _____ (be) lonely.
(2) You will _____ (do) your math homework.

6 should / shouldn't
(1) Your eyes are red. You _____ (rub) them.
(2) You _____ (call) him back. He is waiting for you.

B 「May I ~?」 또는 「Must I ~?」와 괄호 안의 동사를 이용하여 대화를 완성하세요.

1 A: _____ _____ _____ your computer? (use)

B: Sure. Here you go.

2 A: _____ _____ _____? (wait)

B: Yes, you must.

3 A: _____ _____ _____ to you for a second? (talk)

B: I'm sorry, but I don't have time.

4 A: _____ _____ _____ this paper today? (finish)

B: No, you don't have to.

C 뜻이 통하도록 두 문장을 바르게 짝지으세요.

1 Daniel hasn't called me   •
since last week.
                                • (a) He can't be hungry.

2 Ruben studied hard   •
and passed the exam.
                                • (b) He may be busy.

3 Tommy has just had lunch.   •
                                • (c) He must be very happy.

WRITING PRACTICE

우리말과 일치하도록 [보기]와 괄호 안의 동사를 이용하여 문장을 완성하세요.

[보기]   can't   may   should

1 A: 제가 당신의 티켓을 좀 봐도 될까요?   B: 그럼요. (see)

→ A: _____?   B: Of course.

2 매 끼니 후에 양치질해야 한다. (brush)

→ You _____ after each meal.

3 그것이 사실일 리가 없어. 난 믿지 않아. (true)

→ _____. I don't believe it.

☑ CHECK UP **괄호 안에서 알맞은 것을 고르세요.**

1 My glasses (breaks / are broken).　　　　　　　　　　　　　A-1

2 This road (is not used / not is used) very often.　　　　　　　B-1

3 (Does English speak / Is English spoken) in your country?　　B-2

4 This building (is built / was built) in 1999.　　　　　　　　　C-1

5 The work (must be done / must is done) by tomorrow.　　　　C-2

A　　**주어진 말을 알맞은 형태로 바꾸어 능동태 문장과 수동태 문장을 완성하세요. (현재시제로 쓸 것)**

1 write
(1) Jason _____ poems.
(2) This book _____ in Chinese.

2 make
(1) My mom _____ delicious sandwiches.
(2) These carpets _____ in India.

3 clean
(1) The bathroom _____ every morning.
(2) I _____ my room on Saturdays.

4 speak
(1) French _____ in Quebec, Canada.
(2) Jin _____ Korean and Japanese.

5 visit
(1) We _____ our grandparents every month.
(2) The blog _____ by thousands of people every day.

B [보기]에서 알맞은 동사를 골라 적절한 형태로 바꾸어 빈칸을 완성하세요. (과거시제로 쓸 것)

[보기] steal   discover   invite   hit

1 His wallet _____ _____.

2 A car _____ _____ by a truck.

3 America _____ _____ by Columbus.

4 We _____ _____ to a party last night.

C 밑줄 친 부분 중 어법상 옳은 것에 ○ 표시하고, 옳지 않은 것은 바르게 고쳐 쓰세요.

1 The door is not locked.   _____

2 *The Kiss* painted by Gustav Klimt.   _____

3 The game can watch online.   _____

4 Was the light bulb invented by Edison?   _____

5 Will this project completed by March?   _____

6 Some plants can be found only in a special area.   _____

WRITING PRACTICE

우리말과 일치하도록 괄호 안의 말을 바르게 배열하여 문장을 완성하세요.

1 우유가 매일 아침 배달된다. (delivered, the milk, is)

→ _____ every morning.

2 이 사진들은 유럽에서 찍혔다. (taken, these photos, were)

→ _____ in Europe.

3 그 책은 많은 사람들에 의해 읽히지 않았다. (read, by, was, many people, not)

→ The book _____.

4 그 축제는 다음 달에 개최될 것이다. (be, next month, held, will, the festival)

→ _____.

실전 TEST 03 Unit 12-18

[1-3] 다음 빈칸에 들어갈 말로 알맞은 것을 고르세요.

1 The moon _____ around the Earth.

① go ② goes
③ went ④ has gone
⑤ going

2 They _____ on the stage now.

① dance ② danced
③ is dancing ④ are dancing
⑤ have danced

3 A: Have you been to Italy?
B: No, I _____.

① don't ② wasn't ③ didn't
④ haven't ⑤ been not

서술형

4 다음 괄호 안의 말을 알맞은 형태로 바꾸어 대화를 완성하세요.

A: _____ you _____
_____ _____ that
camera? (be going to, buy)
B: No, I'm not. It's too expensive.

[5-8] 다음 밑줄 친 부분 중 어법상 옳지 <u>않은</u> 것을 고르세요.

5 ① I <u>am going</u> to the library.
② We <u>are having</u> dinner now.
③ The man <u>are driving</u> his car fast.
④ Mom <u>is washing</u> the dishes.
⑤ They <u>are drinking</u> tea.

6 ① Sarah <u>studied</u> art in college.
② We <u>had</u> a nice dinner together.
③ I <u>met</u> him on the street this morning.
④ Mr. Lee <u>teached</u> us Korean history.
⑤ I <u>got</u> his e-mail yesterday.

7 ① Koreans <u>eat</u> kimchi a lot.
② They <u>played</u> football yesterday.
③ We <u>did</u> our homework together last night.
④ Sandra and I <u>planned</u> the trip a month ago.
⑤ I <u>take</u> a taxi to school this morning.

8 ① Your computer <u>can be fixed</u>.
② Her purse <u>was stolen</u> yesterday.
③ The island <u>visited</u> by many people.
④ The work <u>will be done</u> next week.
⑤ Was this picture <u>painted</u> by Vincent van Gogh?

서술형

9 다음 빈칸에 동사 **have**를 각각 알맞은 형태로 바꾸어 쓰세요.

> (1) Kelly _____ three dogs now.
> (2) I _____ an important meeting yesterday.

10 다음 짝지어진 두 문장의 뜻이 일치하지 <u>않는</u> 것을 고르세요.

① Can I see your ticket?
  – May I see your ticket?
② You must be here by 9 a.m.
  – You have to be here by 9 a.m.
③ I couldn't get up early today.
  – I wasn't able to get up early today.
④ You must not swim here.
  – You don't have to swim here.
⑤ Tony can't come to the party.
  – Tony is not able to come to the party.

11 다음 중 밑줄 친 부분의 뜻이 나머지와 <u>다른</u> 하나를 고르세요.

① I'm <u>going to</u> learn Chinese.
② Emily <u>is going to</u> join our team.
③ We <u>are going to</u> the museum now.
④ I <u>am going to</u> finish this book this week.
⑤ The restaurant <u>is going to</u> close next month.

서술형

[12-13] 다음 괄호 안의 동사를 알맞은 형태로 바꾸어 대화를 완성하세요.

12

> A: What is Jenny doing?
> B: She _____ _____ (make) cookies.

13

> A: Where does your brother live?
> B: He _____ (live) in New York.

[14-15] 다음 빈칸에 공통으로 들어갈 알맞은 말을 고르세요.

14

> A: When _____ she in Seoul?
> B: She _____ in Seoul four years ago.

① am   ② are   ③ is
④ was   ⑤ were

15

> • They _____ be twins.
> • You _____ finish the report today.

① should   ② are able to
③ will   ④ must
⑤ are going to

16 A: Could I talk to you for a moment?

B : _____

① Sure.   ② Certainly.
③ Of course.   ④ No, I can't.
⑤ I'm sorry, but you can't.

17 A: What did you do last weekend?

B : _____

① I went to the mountain.
② I played baseball with friends.
③ I watched some movies.
④ I read comic books.
⑤ I visit my grandparents.

18 다음 두 문장이 같은 뜻이 되도록 빈칸에 알맞은 말을 고르세요.

Cindy and I met in 2005. We are still friends.
= We have been friends _____ 2005.

① ago   ② for
③ since   ④ just
⑤ already

19 ① I have been to that restaurant three times.
② We have lived in this city for 15 years.
③ Jack has seen the movie twice.
④ They have left ten minutes ago.
⑤ She has gone to Paris.

20 ① I hasn't met Mr. Jones before.
② We have not seen him for a year.
③ Nora hasn't left home yet.
④ They haven't finished the project yet.
⑤ Kevin has never eaten raw fish.

21 A: Were these pictures take in Hawaii?
         ①   ②
B : No, they weren't. I took them on
              ③   ④
Jeju-do. I really like them.
                      ⑤

22 다음 밑줄 친 부분 중 어법상 옳은 것을 고르세요.

① Mike go to bed at 10 p.m.
② I was writing an e-mail now.
③ We have pizza last night.
④ It will be snow tomorrow.
⑤ Andy has been in Seoul since January.

23 다음 중 밑줄 친 **can**의 쓰임이 [보기]와 같은 것을 고르세요.

> [보기] You <u>can</u> use my cell phone.

① Peter <u>can</u> cook bulgogi.
② <u>Can</u> I turn the light on?
③ I <u>can't</u> fix the car.
④ The answer <u>cannot</u> be wrong.
⑤ <u>Can</u> you give us some advice?

24 다음 중 밑줄 친 부분의 성격이 나머지와 **다른** 하나를 고르세요.

① The window <u>is broken</u>.
② My father <u>is busy</u> all the time.
③ I <u>am invited</u> to John's wedding.
④ The newspaper <u>is delivered</u> at 6 a.m.
⑤ This building <u>is cleaned</u> every morning.

[25-26] 다음 중 어법상 옳지 **않은** 것을 고르세요.

25 ① Was she at home?
② Were they friendly?
③ Did you and Edward love each other?
④ Did you know about the quiz?
⑤ When did the movie started?

26 ① He was kind to me.
② It was expensive.
③ I was busy this morning.
④ Tommy was a cook in that restaurant.
⑤ They was middle school students two years ago.

[27-30] 다음 우리말과 일치하도록 괄호 안의 동사를 알맞은 형태로 바꾸어 문장을 완성하세요.

27

> 그 영화에 대해 너에게 말하지 않을게. (tell)

→ I _____ _____ you about the movie.

28

> 넌 돈을 낼 필요 없어. 내가 낼게. (pay)

→ You _____ _____ _____ _____. I'll pay for you.

29

> 이 다리는 100년 전에 지어졌다. (build)

→ This bridge _____ _____ 100 years ago.

30

> 한글은 1443년에 세종대왕에 의해 발명되었다. (invent)

→ Hangul _____ _____ by King Sejong in 1443.

UNIT 19 형용사

↗ CHECK UP **괄호 안에서 알맞은 것을 고르세요.**

1 Andy is (health / healthy).　　　　　　　　　A-2

2 Did you see (strange anything / anything strange)?　　B-1

3 There aren't (much / many) books on the shelf.　　C-1

4 I have (little / few) time now.　　　　　　　C-2

5 I don't have (any / some) sisters.　　　　　　C-3

A **예시와 같이 밑줄 친 부분을 꾸며주거나 보충 설명해주는 말에 동그라미 치세요.**

0 Natasha is a (beautiful) woman.

1 Many people are invited to the party.

2 I'll take this skirt.

3 It looks delicious.

4 The song made him famous.

5 I want to have something spicy.

B **둘 중 알맞은 말을 골라 빈칸을 채우세요.**

1 many / much

(1) She drank too _____ coffee.

(2) He doesn't know _____ songs.

2 a little / a few

(1) You should add _____ salt to this soup.

(2) I'm going to ask _____ questions.

3 little / few

(1) We have _____ money now.

(2) Joan made _____ mistakes on her essay.

C   그림과 일치하도록 [보기 1]과 [보기 2]에서 알맞은 말을 하나씩 골라 문장을 완성하세요.

[보기 1]   big   happy   nice   wrong
[보기 2]   anything   her   eyes   day

1

It's a _____ _____.

2

I can't find _____ _____.

3

The present made _____
_____.

4

Amy has _____ _____.

WRITING PRACTICE

우리말과 일치하도록 괄호 안의 말을 바르게 배열하여 문장을 완성하세요.

1 나는 뭔가 큰 것을 보았다. (big, saw, something, I)

→ _____.

2 너 오늘 피곤해 보여. (today, you, tired, look)

→ _____.

3 그녀는 오늘 아침에 요거트를 조금 먹었다. (ate, yogurt, some, she)

→ _____ this morning.

4 우리는 매일 많은 음식을 낭비한다. (food, we, a lot of, waste)

→ _____ every day.

정답 및 해설 p.33

☑ CHECK UP **괄호 안에서 알맞은 것을 고르세요.**

1 (Lucky / Luckily), he got a ticket. `A-2`

2 David runs (fast / fastly). `A-2`

3 I spent (near / nearly) $ 1,000. `A-2`

4 She (usually has / has usually) lunch with Lisa. `C`

5 I (will never / never will) lie to you again. `C`

A **예시와 같이 밑줄 친 부사가 꾸며주는 말에 동그라미 치세요.**

0 The bus (stopped) suddenly.

1 James is a <u>very</u> handsome guy.

2 You should read the message <u>really</u> carefully.

3 <u>Surprisingly</u>, Sam has already left.

4 The old ladies walked <u>slowly</u>.

5 This room is <u>too</u> hot.

6 He lost a lot of weight <u>very</u> quickly.

7 My grandmother cooks <u>well</u>.

8 <u>Sadly</u>, someone stole my bicycle.

B **두 문장이 같은 뜻이 되도록 밑줄 친 형용사를 알맞은 형태로 바꾸어 빈칸을 완성하세요.**

1 Jim speaks <u>perfect</u> Chinese.

= Jim speaks Chinese _____.

2 She has a <u>gentle</u> smile.

= She smiles _____.

3 We're having <u>heavy</u> rain.

= It's raining _____.

C   둘 중 알맞은 말을 골라 빈칸을 채우세요.

1 late / lately
   (1) You came _____ again!
   (2) He hasn't talked to me _____.

2 hard / hardly
   (1) I can _____ understand the question.
   (2) We studied _____ for the exam.

3 high / highly
   (1) The birds are flying _____.
   (2) That was a _____ dangerous mission.

D   밑줄 친 빈도부사의 위치가 옳으면 ○, 틀리면 × 표시하세요.

1 Ben <u>often</u> plays basketball with his friends.   _____
2 I am <u>sometimes</u> sad.   _____
3 You <u>always</u> should carry your key.   _____
4 I use <u>usually</u> a black pen.   _____
5 He will <u>never</u> remember my name.   _____

WRITING PRACTICE

우리말과 일치하도록 [보기]와 괄호 안의 말을 이용하여 문장을 완성하세요.

[보기]   often   quite   always

1 이 이야기는 꽤 단순하다. (simple)
   → _____

2 나는 항상 일찍 일어난다. (get up)
   → _____

3 우리는 자주 도서관에 간다. (go)
   → _____

UNIT 21 비교

☑ **CHECK UP** **괄호 안에서 알맞은 것을 고르세요.**

1 Love is the (most important / importantest) thing.　　A-1

2 Your idea is (gooder / better) than mine.　　A-2

3 Our team is (very / much) stronger than theirs.　　B

4 He is the smartest boy (in / of) my class.　　C

5 I can run as fast (as / than) you.　　D

A　**그림과 일치하도록 형용사의 비교급 또는 최상급 형태를 써서 빈칸을 완성하세요.**

1

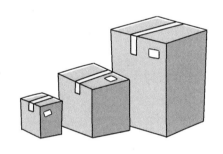

big — _____ — _____

2

little — _____ — _____

3

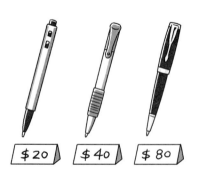

expensive — _____ — _____

4

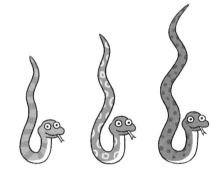

long — _____ — _____

B   괄호 안의 말을 비교급 또는 최상급 중 알맞은 형태로 바꾸어 빈칸을 완성하세요.

1 I am _____ than you. (old)

2 She has the _____ hair of the students. (long)

3 August is the _____ month in Korea. (hot)

4 This is the _____ restaurant in the city. (good)

5 The train is _____ than a bus. (comfortable)

6 This is the _____ building in our town. (new)

7 Jane is _____ than her mother. (tall)

8 He is the _____ singer in Korea. (popular)

C   두 문장이 같은 뜻이 되도록 빈칸에 알맞은 말을 쓰세요.

1 This book is thinner than the dictionary.

= The dictionary is not as _____ as this book.

2 Your car is nicer than mine.

= My car is _____ _____ than yours.

3 He exercises less often than me.

= He doesn't exercise as _____ _____ me.

WRITING PRACTICE

우리말과 일치하도록 괄호 안의 말을 바르게 배열하여 문장을 완성하세요.

1 영어가 수학보다 더 재미있다. (interesting, than, more)

→ English is _____ math.

2 내가 가능한 한 빨리 갈게. (soon, as, possible, as)

→ I'll go _____.

3 내 차는 네 것만큼 크지 않다. (as, yours, not, my car, as, is, big)

→ _____.

☑ CHECK UP   **괄호 안에서 알맞은 것을 고르세요.**

1 Mike sat in front of (I / me). `A-1`

2 Ann and I met (at / on) the airport. `B`

3 The bag (on / around) the sofa is mine. `B`

4 There is a bridge (over / under) the river. `B`

5 It takes an hour (from / between) here to City Hall. `B`

A   **그림과 일치하도록 [보기]에서 알맞은 말을 골라 빈칸을 채우세요.**

[보기]   beside   on   over   under

1 There is a box _____ the desk.

2 There is a pen _____ the desk.

3 There is a bookshelf _____ the desk.

4 There is a fan _____ the desk.

[보기]   between   across from   next to

5 The shoe store is _____ the restaurant.

6 The bank is _____ the library and the shoe store.

7 The bookstore is _____ the school.

B 그림과 일치하도록 빈칸에 알맞은 전치사를 쓰세요.

1

The children are climbing _____ the ladder.

2

He is putting his cell phone _____ the bag.

3

There are many trees _____ his office.

4

She is running _____ the mountain.

WRITING PRACTICE

우리말과 일치하도록 [보기]와 괄호 안의 말을 이용하여 문장을 완성하세요.

[보기] from/to   at   out of   in front of

1 그는 그 호텔에서 지내고 있다. (the hotel)

→ He is staying _____.

2 모든 사람들이 그 건물 밖으로 뛰어나왔다. (the building)

→ All the people ran _____.

3 우리 집에서 학교까지 2km이다. (my home, the school)

→ It is 2 km _____.

4 그녀는 거울 앞에 서 있다. (a mirror)

→ She is standing _____.

☑ CHECK UP   **괄호 안에서 알맞은 것을 고르세요.**

1 I left home (at / in) 8 o'clock this morning.   `A - 1`

2 Bob works (from / since) 9 a.m. to 6 p.m.   `A - 3`

3 You have to write the report (by / until) tomorrow.   `A - 4`

4 The movie was (about / of) war.   `B - 1`

5 I went to the movies (by / with) Dan yesterday.   `B - 5`

A   **빈칸에 in, on, at 중 알맞은 전치사를 쓰세요.**

1 We are going to meet _____ noon.

2 It's warm here _____ spring.

3 We usually eat lunch _____ 12:30.

4 Let's go to the concert _____ Sunday.

5 John will go to Canada _____ September.

6 Mary will have a party _____ her birthday.

B   **[보기]에서 알맞은 말을 하나씩 골라 빈칸을 채우세요.**

[보기]   about   after   by   for   from   until

1 We'll go shopping _____ school.

2 Paul didn't go to bed _____ midnight.

3 This book is _____ Korean history.

4 She waited _____ her boyfriend outside the house.

5 I was in the library _____ 10 a.m. to 5 p.m. yesterday.

6 You must arrive _____ 9:30 because the train leaves at 9:45.

C   빈칸에 공통으로 들어갈 전치사를 쓰세요.

1 He bought flowers _____ me.

I have known them _____ seven years.

2 Finish the work _____ tomorrow.

Can I pay _____ credit card?

3 He cut the bread _____ the knife.

I ate dinner _____ my family yesterday.

D   문장의 밑줄 친 전치사를 바르게 고쳐 쓰세요.

1 The concert is <u>in</u> December 24th.   _____

2 This picture was painted <u>of</u> a famous artist.   _____

3 Mina drew this picture <u>by</u> colored pencils.   _____

4 They went to the airport <u>on</u> subway.   _____

WRITING PRACTICE

우리말과 일치하도록 [보기]와 괄호 안의 말을 이용하여 문장을 완성하세요.

[보기]   during   before   for   without

1 제인은 사흘 동안 프랑스어를 배웠다. (three days)

→ Jane learned French _____.

2 식사 전에 손을 씻어라. (meals)

→ Wash your hands _____.

3 그는 아무 도움 없이 그것을 했다. (any help)

→ _____.

4 너는 여름 방학 동안 무엇을 했니? (summer vacation)

→ _____?

실전 TEST 04 Unit 19-23

[1-2] 다음 중 품사가 <u>다른</u> 하나를 고르세요.

1 ① friendly　② soft　③ quiet
   ④ gently　⑤ funny

2 ① lovely　② very　③ never
   ④ almost　⑤ loudly

3 다음 중 형용사와 부사의 형태가 <u>다른</u> 것을 고르세요.
   ① late　② early　③ enough
   ④ nice　⑤ hard

4 다음 중 부사의 종류가 <u>다른</u> 하나를 고르세요.
   ① always　② often　③ quickly
   ④ usually　⑤ rarely

5 다음 중 밑줄 친 형용사의 역할이 [보기]와 같은 것을 고르세요.

   [보기]　My sister is <u>cute</u>.

   ① You did a <u>good</u> job.
   ② John looks <u>happy</u> today.
   ③ I want something <u>sweet</u>.
   ④ That <u>tall</u> boy is my brother.
   ⑤ We live in a <u>big</u> house.

6 다음 빈칸에 들어갈 수 <u>없는</u> 것을 고르세요.

   He didn't spend _____ money.

   ① much　② any　③ many
   ④ a lot of　⑤ lots of

[7-8] 다음 짝지어진 두 단어의 관계가 나머지와 <u>다른</u> 하나를 고르세요.

7 ① lucky – luckily
   ② good – well
   ③ love – lovely
   ④ loud – loudly
   ⑤ slow – slowly

8 ① safe – safer
   ② little – less
   ③ soon – sooner
   ④ many – most
   ⑤ important – more important

9 다음 빈칸에 공통으로 들어갈 알맞은 말을 고르세요.

   I need _____ milk. I also should
   buy _____ eggs.

   ① some　② a little　③ a few
   ④ many　⑤ much

10 다음 중 밑줄 친 말 앞에 **very**가 들어갈 수 <u>없는</u> 것을 고르세요.

① The movie was <u>interesting</u>.
② She speaks English <u>well</u>.
③ They are <u>famous</u> singers.
④ He told us the story <u>slowly</u>.
⑤ Terry is <u>smarter</u> than me.

11 다음 중 형용사의 원급-비교급-최상급이 바르게 연결된 것을 고르세요.

① thin – thiner – thinest
② happy – happyer – happyest
③ careful – carefuller – carefullest
④ bad – worse – worst
⑤ nice – more nice – most nice

서술형

12 다음 빈칸에 공통으로 들어갈 말을 쓰세요.

> • Put the book _____ the desk.
> • We'll leave _____ Saturday.

13 다음 중 밑줄 친 부사가 꾸며주는 단어의 품사가 나머지와 <u>다른</u> 하나를 고르세요.

① He solved the problem <u>easily</u>.
② The door opened <u>suddenly</u>.
③ Thomas sings <u>well</u>.
④ She smiled very <u>brightly</u>.
⑤ This room is <u>very</u> dark.

[14-16] 다음 빈칸에 들어갈 전치사가 바르게 짝지어진 것을 고르세요.

14
• My feet are smallest _____ my class.
• He runs the fastest _____ all his friends.

① in – as
② of – in
③ as – than
④ in – of
⑤ as – of

15
• Joe came to Korea _____ 2003.
• I arrived home _____ 6 o'clock.

① at – in
② on – at
③ in – at
④ on – in
⑤ in – on

16
It takes 10 minutes _____ my home _____ my school.

① in – to
② from – to
③ at – to
④ from – on
⑤ from – at

17 ① She looks much healthier than before.

② I drive less carefully than him.

③ Jeremy is the best swimmer in my school.

④ Toronto is the biggest city in Canada.

⑤ Your car is as newer as mine.

18 ① Mary has a cute dog.

② He is a good friend.

③ Did you see the red bag?

④ We helped the old lady.

⑤ I don't know famous anyone.

19 ① I exercised during an hour.

② Let's think about the problem.

③ He forgot the title of the book.

④ Max waited until 8 p.m.

⑤ Mr. Brown sang with us.

20 다음 두 문장이 같은 뜻이 되도록 빈칸에 알맞은 말을 쓰세요.

Busan is warmer than Seoul.
= Seoul is not _____ _____
_____ Busan.

[21-22] 다음 표를 보고, 물음에 답하세요.

	Bart	Tom	Eric
height	160 cm	160 cm	170 cm
weight	50 kg	63 kg	78 kg

21 다음 중 표의 내용과 일치하지 않는 것을 고르세요.

① Bart is as tall as Tom.

② Tom is less tall than Eric.

③ Eric is taller than Bart.

④ Eric is not taller than Tom.

⑤ Eric is the tallest of the three boys.

22 표의 내용과 일치하도록 형용사 heavy를 알맞은 형태로 바꾸어 빈칸을 완성하세요.

(1) Eric is much _____ than Bart.
(2) Bart is less _____ than Tom.

23 다음 중 밑줄 친 부사의 위치가 옳지 않은 것을 고르세요.

① He often is late for school.

② I never tell lies.

③ You sometimes look unhappy.

④ She usually drives to work.

⑤ Sam always gets up at 7.

24 다음 중 형용사를 부사로 바꾼 것이 옳지 <u>않은</u> 것을 고르세요.

① simple → simply

② true → truly

③ busy → busily

④ full → fully

⑤ enough → enoughly

서술형

[25-27] 다음 우리말과 일치하도록 빈칸에 알맞은 말을 써서 대화를 완성하세요.

25

> A : 나 감기에 걸렸어.
>
> I got a cold.
>
> B : 그럼 물을 많이 마시렴.
>
> Then, drink _____ _____ _____ water.

26

> A : 너는 일찍 잠자리에 드니?
>
> Do you go to bed early?
>
> B : 아니, 나는 보통 꽤 늦게 잠자리에 들어.
>
> No, I _____ go to bed quite _____.

27

> A : 네 시계가 내 것보다 더 비싸.
>
> Your watch is _____ _____ than mine.
>
> B : 하지만 네 시계도 내 것만큼 좋아.
>
> But your watch is _____ good _____ mine.

28 다음 빈칸에 들어갈 말이 바르게 짝지어진 것을 고르세요.

> There isn't _____ milk. You can have _____ juice.

① some − any

② any − many

③ a few − some

④ many − much

⑤ any − some

29 다음 짝지어진 두 문장의 뜻이 일치하지 <u>않는</u> 것을 고르세요.

① She is a good cook.

　- She cooks well.

② He speaks perfect Chinese.

　- He speaks Chinese perfectly.

③ I am a fast learner.

　- I learn fast.

④ I was late for school.

　- I got to school lately.

⑤ Paul is a careful driver.

　- Paul drives carefully.

30 다음 중 밑줄 친 부분의 역할이 나머지와 <u>다른</u> 하나를 고르세요.

① I know the man <u>in the room</u>.

② The dog <u>under the bed</u> is mine.

③ We met <u>at the park</u>.

④ Help the lady <u>with the big bag</u>.

⑤ You can eat the cake <u>on the plate</u>.

☑ CHECK
UP

괄호 안에서 알맞은 것을 고르세요.

1 My father decided (to not smoke / not to smoke). `A-1`

2 It is dangerous (go out / to go out) alone at night. `B-1`

3 I want (buy / to buy) new jeans. `B-2`

4 Jack's goal is (play / to play) the guitar well. `B-3`

5 He asked me (do / to do) the work. `B-3`

A **[보기]에서 알맞은 동사를 골라 to부정사로 바꾸어 빈칸을 완성하세요.**

[보기]   learn   watch   solve   protect

1 It was difficult _____ _____ this puzzle.

2 It was fun _____ _____ the show.

3 It is important _____ _____ the environment.

4 It is interesting _____ _____ foreign languages.

B **밑줄 친 to부정사가 명사, 형용사, 부사 중 어떤 역할을 하는지 쓰세요.**

1 I like to go to the movies. _____

2 It is fun to visit new places. _____

3 It was easy to get to the airport. _____

4 His wish is to lose seven kilograms. _____

5 They decided to travel to India. _____

6 Dorothy wants to learn Korean. _____

7 Everyone needs someone to trust. _____

8 Do you have anything to say? _____

C   그림과 일치하도록 괄호 안의 동사를 이용하여 빈칸을 완성하세요.

1

I _____ _____ _____
you again. (hope, see)

2

I _____ _____ _____ a
writer. (want, be)

3

My parents _____ _____
_____ a car. (decided, buy)

4

Peter _____ _____
_____ home by eight.
(promised, come)

WRITING PRACTICE

우리말과 일치하도록 괄호 안의 말을 바르게 배열하여 문장을 완성하세요.

1 나는 지금 당장 아무것도 먹고 싶지 않다. (to, want, eat, don't)

→ I _____ anything right now.

2 나의 계획은 매일 한 시간씩 운동하는 것이다. (exercise, is, my plan, to)

→ _____ for an hour every day.

3 진정한 친구를 사귀는 것은 어렵다. (difficult, true, friends, to, it, is, make)

→ _____ .

4 나는 그것들을 어디서 사야 할지 못 찾겠다. (buy, where, them, to)

→ I can't find _____ .

☑ CHECK
   UP

괄호 안에서 알맞은 것을 고르세요.

1 I have something (tell / to tell) you.   A

2 He called me (to ask / and ask) about the project.   B-1

3 I am glad (see / to see) you again.   B-2

4 His words are hard (understand / to understand).   B-3

5 Mary was (too / so) busy to eat lunch.   C

A

밑줄 친 to부정사가 형용사와 부사 중 어떤 역할을 하는지 빈칸에 번호를 쓰세요.

1 I was happy to hear from you.

2 Eric has lots of things to do.

3 I don't have time to read the book.

4 The song is impossible to sing.

5 I came here to meet Mr. Jeong.

6 I have homework to finish.

7 Jane was sad to hear the bad news.

8 He is saving money to buy a bike.

• 형용사 역할: _____   • 부사 역할: _____

B

밑줄 친 부사 역할을 하는 to부정사가 '목적'과 '원인' 중 어떤 뜻을 나타내는지 쓰세요.

1 Tom went to the library to find the book.   _____

2 We were happy to see him again.   _____

3 Bob studied hard to pass the exam.   _____

4 They were shocked to see their bill.   _____

5 I was sad to break up with my girlfriend.   _____

6 He turned on the TV to watch the football game.   _____

C 　그림과 일치하도록 [보기]에서 동사를 하나씩 골라 적절한 형태로 바꾸어 빈칸을 완성하세요.

[보기]　wear　　drink　　hear　　stay

1

She was surprised _____
_____ the news.

2

The shirt is too small _____
_____ .

3

They wanted something _____
_____ .

4

It is warm enough _____
_____ outside.

WRITING PRACTICE

우리말과 일치하도록 괄호 안의 동사를 이용하여 문장을 완성하세요.

1 라면은 요리하기 쉽다. (cook)

→ Ramyeon is _____ .

2 네게 보여줄 사진이 몇 장 있다. (show)

→ I have some pictures _____ .

3 수영하기에 너무 춥다. (swim)

→ It is _____ .

UNIT 26 동명사

☑ CHECK UP   **괄호 안에서 알맞은 것을 고르세요.**

1 (Lying / Lieing) to children is wrong.   A

2 (Lose / Losing) weight is difficult.   B-1

3 She wants (traveling / to travel) to Europe.   B-2

4 How about (having / to have) fried chicken?   B-2

5 My bad habit is (bite / biting) my nails.   B-3

A **두 문장이 같은 뜻이 되도록 빈칸에 알맞은 말을 쓰세요.**

1 It is a good idea to drink a lot of water.

= _____ a lot of water is a good idea.

2 Peter started to learn yoga yesterday.

= Peter started _____ yoga yesterday.

3 I like to watch baseball games.

= I like _____ baseball games.

4 Her job is to teach English.

= Her job is _____ English.

B **[보기]에서 알맞은 동사를 하나씩 골라 적절한 형태로 바꾸어 빈칸을 완성하세요.**

[보기]   go   see   send   play   eat

1 I enjoy _____ badminton.

2 Ms. Kim wants _____ you now.

3 I have decided not _____ chocolate.

4 Would you mind _____ me the image file?

5 We decided _____ to the museum next week.

C 그림과 일치하도록 괄호 안의 동사를 알맞은 형태로 바꾸어 빈칸을 완성하세요.

1

_____ is good for your health. (laugh)

2

I finished _____ the house. (clean)

3

This book is about _____ cookies. (bake)

4

I plan _____ my grandparents this Sunday. (visit)

WRITING PRACTICE

우리말과 일치하도록 괄호 안의 말을 바르게 배열하여 문장을 완성하세요.

1 마이크는 노래 부르는 것을 잘한다. (singing, Mike, good, is, at)

→ _____.

2 내 취미는 동전을 모으는 것이다. (collecting, is, coins, my hobby)

→ _____.

3 새로운 언어를 배우는 것은 쉽지 않다. (not, learning, is, easy, a new language)

→ _____.

4 그는 어떻게 담배 피우는 것을 그만두었니? (smoking, did, quit, how, he)

→ _____?

UNIT 27 분사

CHECK UP 괄호 안에서 알맞은 것을 고르세요.

1 Julie has (going / gone) to Spain. A-1

2 It was a (boring / bored) class. A-2

3 James has just (come / coming) home. B-1

4 (Sleeping cats / Cats sleeping) look peaceful. B-2

5 The (man playing / playing man) a guitar is my brother. B-2

A 밑줄 친 분사의 쓰임이 옳으면 ○, 옳지 않으면 × 표시하세요.

1 We saw an <u>excited</u> tennis match yesterday. _____

2 Pavel is <u>dancing</u> to the rock music. _____

3 The pictures were <u>drawn</u> by Egon Schiele. _____

4 The <u>broken</u> glass is dangerous. _____

5 They have <u>lived</u> here for 10 years. _____

B 괄호 안의 동사를 알맞은 분사 형태로 바꾸어 빈칸을 완성하세요.

1 Harry is _____ to school now. (go)

2 It was an _____ concert. (amaze)

3 I have _____ him for ten years. (know)

4 She bought a bag _____ in China. (make)

5 My house was _____ by my grandfather. (build)

6 The woman _____ a book is my teacher. (hold)

7 The baby _____ on the bed is cute. (lie)

8 I am _____ a shower in the bathroom. (take)

9 I read an _____ book last night. (interest)

10 Ice is _____ water. (freeze)

C [보기]에서 알맞은 동사를 하나씩 골라 적절한 형태로 바꾸어 빈칸을 완성하세요.

[보기] close   call   surprise   fall

1 John has a cute cat _____ Chacha.
2 Look at the _____ leaves on the ground.
3 I heard some _____ news this morning.
4 He waited for her in front of the _____ door of her office.

D 문장의 밑줄 친 부분을 바르게 고쳐 쓰세요.

1 It was a very <u>excited</u> movie.   _____
2 There is a tree <u>grown</u> in the garden.   _____
3 The actress <u>is loving</u> by many people.   _____
4 Do you know that <u>wearing girl</u> the red hat?   _____
5 The police found the <u>lose</u> child at the airport. _____

WRITING PRACTICE

우리말과 일치하도록 [보기]와 괄호 안의 말을 이용하여 문장을 완성하세요. ([보기]에서 필요한 단어만 쓸 것)

[보기] writing   written   sleeping   slept   connecting   connected

1 자고 있는 그 강아지를 봐. (the puppy)
→ Look at _____.

2 나는 프랑스어로 쓰인 책을 가지고 있다. (a book, French, in)
→ I have _____.

3 이것은 두 도시를 연결하는 다리이다. (a bridge, this, two cities, is)
→ _____.

실전 TEST 05 Unit 24-27

[1-5] 다음 빈칸에 들어갈 말로 알맞은 것을 고르세요.

1 I decided _____ a music club.

① join   ② joining
③ to join   ④ to joining
⑤ joined

2 Finish _____ your homework.

① do   ② doing
③ to do   ④ to doing
⑤ done

3 I will buy a _____ car.

① use   ② using
③ to use   ④ to used
⑤ used

4 _____ is fun to play baseball.

① It   ② That
③ This   ④ What
⑤ There

5 다음 우리말과 일치하도록 괄호 안의 단어를 배열할 때 ★에 오는 말을 고르세요.

나는 무대에서 춤추는 그 소녀를 사랑한다.
(girl, dancing, the, love, on)
→ I _____ _____ ★ _____
_____ _____ the stage.

① girl   ② dancing   ③ the
④ love   ⑤ on

[6-7] 다음 밑줄 친 부분 중 어법상 옳은 것을 고르세요.

6 ① This is a <u>bored</u> novel.
② He decided <u>to smoke not</u>.
③ How about <u>take</u> a walk?
④ She quit <u>eating</u> fast food.
⑤ I heard a <u>surprised</u> story from them.

7 ① I am <u>washed</u> dishes.
② I don't know <u>how playing</u> the game.
③ I like the sound of the <u>fallen</u> rain.
④ Andy enjoys <u>to watch</u> talk shows.
⑤ My favorite activity is <u>drawing</u> pictures.

8 다음 중 밑줄 친 부분의 성격이 나머지와 다른 하나를 고르세요.

① They are <u>watching</u> TV now.
② She is <u>talking</u> on the phone.
③ My hobby is <u>making</u> model planes.
④ The man <u>wearing</u> a red tie is my father.
⑤ I watched an <u>exciting</u> movie yesterday.

9 다음 빈칸에 들어갈 말이 바르게 짝지어진 것을 고르세요.

> A: Would you mind _____ me?
> B: Sorry, I can't. I have a lot of things _____.

① helping – doing
② helping – to do
③ to help – doing
④ to help – to do
⑤ helping – to doing

[10-11] 다음 중 밑줄 친 부분의 역할이 나머지와 다른 하나를 고르세요.

10 ① He plans to buy a house.
② I like to cook for people.
③ His wish is to meet her again.
④ She was happy to pass the exam.
⑤ Her dream is to become an actor.

11 ① We want something to drink.
② He has a lot of homework to do.
③ It is difficult to make kimchi.
④ I don't have any books to read.
⑤ She has no friends to help her.

서술형

[12-13] 다음 두 문장이 같은 뜻이 되도록 빈칸에 알맞은 말을 쓰세요.

12
> Tony likes helping others.
> = Tony likes _____ _____ others.

13
> Eating too much sugar is not good.
> = _____ is not good _____ _____ too much sugar.

[14-15] 다음 우리말을 영어로 바르게 옮긴 것을 고르세요.

14 그 영화는 10년 전에 만들어졌다.

① The movie was make 10 years ago.
② The movie was made 10 years ago.
③ The movie was making 10 years ago.
④ The movie was to make 10 years ago.
⑤ The movie was to making 10 years ago.

15 그는 그 건물을 살 수 있을 정도로 부유하다.

① He is too rich to buy the building.
② He is too rich buying the building.
③ He is rich enough buying the building.
④ He is rich enough to buy the building.
⑤ He is enough rich to buy the building.

16 Don't go near the _____ vase.

① break   ② broke
③ broken   ④ breaking
⑤ to break

17 There is a bus _____ tonight.

① leave   ② left
③ leaving   ④ to left
⑤ to leaving

18 Mary hopes _____ a good job.

① get   ② got
③ gotten   ④ to get
⑤ getting

19 He began _____ to us.
(2개)

① lie   ② lied
③ lying   ④ to lying
⑤ to lie

서술형

[20-23] 다음 우리말과 일치하도록 괄호 안의 말을 바르게 배열하여 문장을 완성하세요.

20 나는 사실을 말하지 않는 것을 싫어한다.
(the, telling, not, truth)

→ I hate _____.

21 그의 계획은 매일 수학 공부를 하는 것이다.
(his, is, study, plan, to)

→ _____
math every day.

22 자전거를 타고 있는 저 여자를 아니?
(woman, the bicycle, riding, that)

→ Do you know _____
_____?

23 언제 시작할지 말해줘.
(to, tell, when, start, me)

→ _____
_____.

24 다음 중 [보기]의 밑줄 친 부분과 쓰임이 다른 하나를 고르세요.

> [보기]   You have to bring your sleeping bag.

① Writing a book is interesting.
② Julia likes cooking for her family.
③ The singing birds are too noisy.
④ The lesson is about learning how to think.
⑤ Peter enjoys dancing with his friends.

[25-26] 다음 밑줄 친 부분 중 어법상 옳지 않은 것을 고르세요.

25 ① I plan to travel around Europe.
② He wants to buy a nice car.
③ I avoid going shopping on weekends.
④ Do you mind opening the door?
⑤ James finished to read the magazine.

26 ① I have just heard the news.
② The girl playing the violin is my sister.
③ I love that man singing a song.
④ I have some surprised news for you.
⑤ The injured driver is in hospital.

27 다음 중 [보기]의 밑줄 친 부분과 쓰임이 같은 것을 고르세요.

> [보기]   I went to the store to buy a present.

① He likes to write love songs.
② It is hard to believe the story.
③ I was angry to hear the news.
④ She went to Tokyo to learn Japanese.
⑤ I don't have time to finish the work.

서술형

[28-30] 다음 우리말과 일치하도록 괄호 안의 말을 이용하여 문장을 완성하세요.

28
> 그 책은 사진을 찍는 것에 관한 것이다.
> (be, about, take)

→ The book _____ _____
_____ pictures.

29
> 나는 중국어로 쓰여진 이메일을 받았다.
> (an e-mail, write)

→ I got _____ _____
_____ in Chinese.

30
> 나는 학교에 가기엔 너무 아팠다. (sick, go)

→ I was _____ _____
_____ _____ to school.

UNIT 28 접속사

☑ CHECK UP

괄호 안에서 알맞은 것을 고르세요.

1 She likes horror movies, (but / so) I don't. `A-2`
2 Which do you want, milk (so / or) juice? `A-3`
3 (When / Before) I was young, I wanted to be a teacher. `B-1`
4 Joe will be happy (if / because) you call him. `B-2`
5 I think (when / that) he is cute. `C-2`

A 밑줄 친 접속사가 연결해주는 말에 각각 동그라미 치세요.

1 Lisa and I are good friends.
2 He played the piano and I played the violin.
3 I can go to your house, or you can come to mine.
4 Should I go or stay?
5 He is young but wise.
6 Amy likes baseball, but I don't.

B 그림과 일치하도록 [보기]에 주어진 말과 접속사 that을 써서 문장을 완성하세요.

[보기]   they will win the game   we could get the tickets
         they don't listen to me

1    2    3

1 The problem is _____.
2 It was great _____.
3 They believe _____.

C [보기]에서 알맞은 말을 하나씩 골라 빈칸을 채우세요.

[보기]   and   but   or   so

1 I ran, _____ I missed the bus.

2 I had chicken _____ rice for dinner.

3 Which do you like, red _____ green?

4 I saved money, _____ I could buy the computer.

D [보기]에서 알맞은 말을 하나씩 골라 문장을 완성하세요.

[보기]   when we went to Paris   if we take a taxi
         before you go to bed   because it was too hot

1 We opened the window _____.

2 You should brush your teeth _____.

3 _____, we'll get there faster.

4 _____, we had a good time.

WRITING PRACTICE

우리말과 일치하도록 [보기]와 괄호 안의 말을 이용하여 문장을 완성하세요.

[보기]   while   and   that

1 우리는 빵과 버터, 잼을 샀다. (bread, butter, jam)

→ We bought _____.

2 나는 집으로 운전하는 동안 라디오로 뉴스를 들었다. (drove)

→ _____ home, I listened to the news on the radio.

3 그가 다음 달에 떠난다는 것은 사실이다. (true)

→ _____ he will leave next month.

☑ CHECK
UP **괄호 안에서 알맞은 것을 고르세요.**

1 I know the man (who / which) built this building. `B`

2 There are some hotels that (have / has) nice rooms. `B`

3 This is the book (who / which) I bought yesterday. `C`

4 The people (who / which) we met were Japanese. `C`

5 Did you hear the news (who / that) Jina told us? `C`

A **예시와 같이 밑줄 친 선행사를 꾸며주는 관계대명사절에 동그라미 치세요.**

0 I met the girl ⟨who lives next door⟩.

1 He is wearing a shirt which is too big for him.

2 The man who is standing at the door is my uncle.

3 French is the language that I learned two years ago.

4 A bakery is a shop that sells bread and cookies.

5 It is the birthday present which Sue gave to me.

6 The old lady who I helped had a heavy bag.

B **관계대명사 who 또는 which를 써서 한 문장으로 만드세요.**

1 Cindy is my friend. I like her the most.

→ Cindy is the friend _____ _____ _____ _____ _____.

2 There are some neighbors. I haven't met them before.

→ There are some neighbors _____ _____ _____ _____

_____.

3 We saw the movie. It was good.

→ The movie _____ _____ _____ was good.

4 Where is the watch? I fixed it yesterday.

→ Where is the watch _____ _____ _____ _____?

C 관계대명사 who 또는 which와, 괄호 안의 동사를 써서 빈칸을 완성하세요. (현재시제로 쓸 것)

1 The teacher _____ math is Mr. Lee. (teach)

2 I have a friend _____ at the library. (work)

3 A dentist is a person _____ care of your teeth. (take)

4 I like stories _____ me laugh. (make)

5 The girl _____ blue eyes is Sally. (have)

D 관계대명사가 생략된 위치에 ✔ 표시하고 생략된 관계대명사를 쓰세요.

1 Jim has the same tennis shoes I have. _____

2 That is the guy I met at the party yesterday. _____

3 I lost the letter I got from her. _____

4 I didn't know the meaning of the word she wrote. _____

WRITING PRACTICE

우리말과 일치하도록 [보기]와 괄호 안의 말을 이용하여 빈칸을 완성하세요.

[보기] who   which   whom

1 너는 잘못된 문장들을 고쳐야 한다. (wrong)

→ You should correct the sentences _____ _____ _____.

2 저 애가 내가 어제 만난 소녀다. (met)

→ That's the girl _____ _____ _____ yesterday.

3 나와 함께 온 남자아이들은 우리 반 친구들이다. (came with)

→ The boys _____ _____ _____ me are my classmates.

UNIT 30 기타 구문

CHECK UP 괄호 안에서 알맞은 것을 고르세요.

1 She is from Argentina, (doesn't / isn't) she? `A-1`

2 Never (go / going) to that restaurant. `B-2`

3 (Let's not / Not let's) go out tonight. `C`

4 How about (swim / swimming) together in the pool? `C`

5 (How / What) cute she is! `D`

A 빈칸에 알맞은 부가의문문을 쓰세요.

1 You have a sister, _____ _____?

2 It isn't funny, _____ _____?

3 Eric wasn't with Jane yesterday, _____ _____?

4 He can play the viola, _____ _____?

5 She came to the party, _____ _____?

6 You will meet her tonight, _____ _____?

B [보기]에서 알맞은 말을 골라 대화를 완성하세요.

[보기]   Never open   Be   Don't buy   Wake up

1 A: I'm driving on the icy roads.

B: _____ careful.

2 A: _____.

B: What time is it?

3 A: _____ this box.

B: Why? What's in it?

4 A: This cake is too expensive.

B: _____ it.

C 괄호 안의 말과 Let's를 이용하여 문장을 완성하세요.

1 It's cold here. _____ _____ the window. (close)

2 I'm full. _____ _____ _____ dessert. (not, order)

3 That looks heavy. _____ _____ her. (help)

4 The class ends at 4. _____ _____ at 5. (meet)

5 It's dark. _____ _____ on the light. (turn)

6 I'm tired. _____ _____ _____ to the party. (not, go)

D 괄호 안의 말을 바르게 배열하여 감탄문을 완성하세요.

1 (pity, a, what)

→ _____!

2 (time, fast, flies, how)

→ _____!

3 (is, she, how, nice)

→ _____!

4 (a, boy, what, is, smart, he)

→ _____!

WRITING PRACTICE

우리말과 일치하도록 괄호 안의 말을 이용하여 문장을 완성하세요.

1 나를 떠나지 않을 거지, 그렇지? (you)

→ You won't leave me, _____ _____?

2 우리 커피 한 잔 할까? (drink)

→ _____ _____ _____ a cup of coffee?

3 우리 함께 저녁 먹는 게 어때? (have)

→ _____ _____ _____ _____ dinner together?

실전 TEST 06 Unit 28-30

[1-3] 다음 우리말과 일치하도록 빈칸에 들어갈 알맞은 말을 고르세요.

1 12살 때 그녀는 세 가지 언어를 말할 수 있었다.
→ _____ she was 12, she could speak three languages.

① After   ② Because
③ If   ④ When
⑤ Before

2 나는 그가 전화하기 전에 점심을 먹었다.
→ I had lunch _____ he called me.

① after   ② because
③ if   ④ when
⑤ before

3 잭이 이 편지를 썼지, 그렇지 않니?
→ Jack wrote this letter, _____ he?

① does   ② did
③ doesn't   ④ didn't
⑤ don't

4 다음 문장에서 ✔ 표시한 부분에 공통으로 생략된 것을 고르세요.

• I think ✔ I lost my key.
• There are a few words ✔ I don't know.

① if   ② so   ③ what
④ that   ⑤ which

5 다음 중 어법상 옳지 않은 것을 고르세요.

① Give me the key, please.
② Never do that again.
③ Why don't we asking her about it?
④ Don't be so shy in front of others.
⑤ What about going for a walk with me?

6 다음 중 밑줄 친 접속사가 적절하지 않은 것을 고르세요.

① Is this comic book yours or his?
② I watched TV after I had lunch.
③ She couldn't go to work if she was sick.
④ It was too expensive, so I didn't buy it.
⑤ He waited for me while I used the bathroom.

[7-8] 다음 빈칸에 들어갈 알맞은 말을 모두 고르세요. (2개)

7 The boy _____ lives next door is my classmate.

① whom   ② who   ③ what
④ which   ⑤ that

8 We liked the movie _____ we saw last night.

① which   ② who   ③ that
④ whom   ⑤ what

9 다음 중 우리말을 영어로 <u>잘못</u> 옮긴 것을 고르세요.

① 나한테 거짓말 그만 해.

- Stop lying to me.

② 우리 도서관에 가자.

- Let's go to the library.

③ 절대 네 꿈을 포기하지 마라.

- Never give up your dream.

④ 우리 바깥에 앉을까?

- Shall we sitting outside?

⑤ 영어로 이야기하는 게 어때?

- Why don't we speak English?

[10-11] 다음 빈칸에 공통으로 들어갈 알맞은 말을 고르세요.

10 • She was cooking _____ he was reading the newspaper.

• I bought some food _____ drinks at the market.

① but ② and ③ so
④ or ⑤ if

11 • It is true _____ Lauren teaches French at school.

• He thinks _____ you are angry with him.

① about ② that ③ because
④ when ⑤ while

[12-13] 다음 빈칸에 들어갈 알맞은 말을 고르세요.

12 The girl _____ is my friend.

① has long hair
② whom have long hair
③ that have long hair
④ who has long hair
⑤ which has long hair

13 It is surprising _____.

① that he passed the exam
② he passed the exam
③ which he passed the exam
④ whom he passed the exam
⑤ who he passed the exam

서술형

[14-15] 다음 우리말과 일치하도록 괄호 안의 말을 이용하여 문장을 완성하세요.

14 그것에 대해서는 말하지 말자. (Let's, talk)

→ _____ _____ _____

about it.

15 넌 정말 친절한 아이로구나! (nice, boy)

→ _____ _____ _____

_____ you are!

16 다음 중 밑줄 친 부분의 역할이 나머지와 다른 하나를 고르세요.

① He thinks <u>that I will come.</u>
② The fact is <u>that he can't swim.</u>
③ Did you know <u>that she was Jenny's sister?</u>
④ I guess <u>that they know the answer.</u>
⑤ We believe <u>that he will get better soon.</u>

[17-18] 다음 빈칸에 들어갈 말이 바르게 짝지어진 것을 고르세요.

17
• She went shopping with her sister, _____ she?
• You won't be angry with me, _____ you?

① doesn't – was
② didn't – are
③ don't – won't
④ didn't – will
⑤ doesn't – will

18
_____ I was sick, I didn't go to school.
= I was sick, _____ I didn't go to school.

① So – when
② After – but
③ Because – so
④ So – because
⑤ Because – that

19 다음 밑줄 친 부분 중 생략할 수 있는 것을 고르세요.

① I know a man <u>who</u> works at the hospital.
② We live in a house <u>which</u> has three rooms.
③ The soup <u>that</u> you made was delicious.
④ Have you seen the book <u>which</u> was on the desk?
⑤ I have a friend <u>who</u> is from Canada.

[20-22] 다음 빈칸에 공통으로 들어갈 알맞은 말을 쓰세요.

20
• He did that for you, _____ he?
• She bought the red coat, _____ she?

21
• _____ a kind person he is!
• _____ great friends (they are)!

22
• _____ about going to the restaurant tonight?
• _____ beautiful these shoes are!

[23-26] 다음 밑줄 친 부분 중 어법상 옳지 <u>않은</u> 것을 고르세요.

23 When I <u>will see</u> you again, I <u>will have</u> so
        ①   ②   ③

many things <u>to tell</u> you.
 ④   ⑤

24 The singer <u>whom</u> <u>I</u> <u>like</u> <u>her</u> the most <u>will</u>
              ① ②③ ④   ⑤

hold her first concert this summer.

25 ① I was happy, but <u>he wasn't</u>.
   ② Do you want chicken or <u>beef</u>?
   ③ She is kind and <u>cute</u>.
   ④ He is strange but <u>funny</u>.
   ⑤ I stayed at home and <u>reading books</u>.

26 ① Where is the bag <u>that I like most</u>?
   ② John stayed at a hotel <u>which were built</u> in 1950.
   ③ The dog <u>that has a long tail</u> is cute.
   ④ I know the girls <u>who are on the stage</u>.
   ⑤ Find the sentences <u>that are wrong</u>.

[27-30] 다음 우리말과 일치하도록 빈칸에 알맞은 말을 써서 문장을 완성하세요.

27 A: 아침을 안 먹어서 배고파.
     I'm hungry _____ I didn't have breakfast.
   B: 수업 전에 간식을 먹는 게 어때?
     Why don't you have a snack before class?

28 A: 면접 때문에 긴장이 돼요.
     I am nervous about the interview.
   B: 두려워하지 마.
     _____ _____ afraid.

29 A: 이름을 적어주세요.
     _____ down your name, _____.
   B: 영어로 써야 하나요?
     Should I write it in English?

30 A: 이 피자 맛이 없어.
     This pizza tastes bad.
   B: 다시는 여기서 먹지 말자.
     _____ _____ eat here again.

지은이

NE능률 영어교육연구소

NE능률 영어교육연구소는 혁신적이며 효율적인 영어 교재를 개발하고
영어 학습의 질을 한 단계 높이고자 노력하는 NE능률의 연구조직입니다.

GRAMMAR ZONE WORKBOOK 〈입문편〉

펴 낸 이 주민홍
펴 낸 곳 서울특별시 마포구 월드컵북로 396(상암동) 누리꿈스퀘어 비즈니스타워 10층
(주)NE능률 (우편번호 03925)
펴 낸 날 2017년 1월 5일 개정판 제1쇄
2023년 4월 15일 제15쇄
전　　화 02 2014 7114
팩　　스 02 3142 0356
홈페이지 www.neungyule.com
등록번호 제 1-68호
I S B N 979-11-253-1235-2 53740
정　　가 6,500원

NE 능률

고객센터

교재 내용 문의 : contact.nebooks.co.kr (별도의 가입 절차 없이 작성 가능)
제품 구매, 교환, 불량, 반품 문의 : 02-2014-7114
☎ 전화문의는 본사 업무시간 중에만 가능합니다.

www.nebooks.co.kr

NE 능률

필수 개념부터 서술형 문제까지 한 권에 多 담았다!

with workbook

GRAMMAR
Inside

LEVEL 2

A 4-level grammar course
with abundant writing practice

A Best-Selling
Grammar
Book

NE_ Neungyule

전국 **온오프 서점** 판매중

중학 영어에 필요한 모든 것 Inside 시리즈

STARTER
(예비중)

LEVEL 1
(중1)

LEVEL 2
(중1-2)

LEVEL 3
(중3)

STARTER
(중1)

LEVEL 1
(중1-2)

LEVEL 2
(중2-3)

LEVEL 3
(중3)

GRAMMAR Inside

· 꼭 알아야 할 중학 영문법 필수 개념만 담아 4단계로 구성
· 많은 양의 문제 풀이로 충분히 연습하여 완벽히 이해
· 서술형 문제를 대폭 수록하여 학교 내신에 철저히 대비
· 풍부한 양의 추가 문제를 수록한 워크북으로 복습 완성

READING Inside

· 문·이과 통합, 타교과 연계 지문이 수록된 원서형 독해서
· 다양한 유형의 질 높은 문제로 내신 및 서술형 시험 대비
· 필수 문법, 어휘, 지문 분석 연습을 위한 코너 수록
· 워크북 추가 문제 풀이로 학습 효과 극대화

www.nebooks.co.kr

NE 능률

기초 세우고 내신 잡는 중학 영어의 첫걸음!

시도 교육청 중학 영어듣기평가 유형별 실전 대비서

NE 능률

1316 팬클럽 듣기

· 기출 문제 수록
· 실전 모의고사 8회분 수록
· 일반 / 빠른 배속 녹음 듣기 파일 제공
  (빠른 배속 듣기는 www.nebooks.co.kr에서 다운로드)

듣기 MP3 파일 무료 다운로드
www.nebooks.co.kr

Level 1

NE능률 영어교육연구소 지음 | 이재언 박진형 박서경

전국 온오프 서점 판매중

단기 완성 중학 내신 기본서 1316팬클럽

독해 LEVEL 1
(초6-예비중)

독해 LEVEL 2
(중1-2)

독해 LEVEL 3
(중2-3)

듣기 LEVEL 1
(중1)

듣기 LEVEL 2
(중2)

듣기 LEVEL 3
(중3)

문법 LEVEL 1
(중1)

문법 LEVEL 2
(중2)

문법 LEVEL 3
(중3)

중학 독해의 시작, 1316팬클럽 독해

· 알찬 40개 지문, 다양한 내신 대비 문제 수록
· QR코드 스캔으로 지문 MP3 파일 간편하게 청취

중학 영어듣기 실전대비서, 1316팬클럽 듣기

· 시·도 교육청 중학 영어듣기평가 유형별 실전 대비
· 최신 영어듣기평가를 반영한 신유형 집중 탐구

내신 잡는 중학 영문법, 1316팬클럽 문법

· 실제 내신 유형과 유사한 문제, 실용적 예문 구성
· 쉽고 명확한 설명으로 내신 핵심 문법 마스터